SUCCESS STRATEGIES FOR IMMIGRANTS

KEYS TO A SUCCESSFUL FUTURE

KATHRYN CANSON

Library and Archives of Canada (LAC)
Title: Success Strategies for Immigrants, Keys to A Successful Future
Format: Hardcover book

ISBN: 978-1-9995087-0-8

This book is dedicated to my Lola Inde who taught me love of reading and learning, my parents Alexander Canson, Sr. and Elizabeth Mahusay Canson, my brothers and sisters Alex, Evans, Daffodil, Samuel, Joshua and Rey my most ardent supporters. To my husband David, thank you for your love and undying belief in me even when many times I doubted myself. Most of all, I thank God Almighty and my Lord Jesus Christ for giving me life and for loving me always and forever.

Contents

PART 4

PART 5

PART 1
Introduction

We dreamed, we risked, we came.

Do you remember the first time you've arrived? The feeling of excitement, hearts beating fast, eyes wide taking in everything. Everything was new. You have new experiences, new places to explore, new people to meet.

Oh! the days of joy when you realized you've arrived at your dream destination.

Then reality sinks in.

Now what should I do? Where should I start? You manage to slowly build your life again in a new country, learning new things and gradually becoming part of a community.

At the back of your mind you have this burning question. Would I be successful? What if I fail? How do I face my family and friends? What would I do if I fail? Can I handle it? Then the resolve comes. "I must not fail".

Success is what we aim for. Anyone who goes to another country hopes and dreams of success. We want better lives for ourselves and our family. But then how do we really go about starting all over again and somehow getting to the top of the mountain we call success? Better yet, how do we define success?

When you are in a strange world (meaning the place you were not born into or in another country) and you don't quite know where to begin, let my voice be your guide and accompany you as you find your way. You are at the center of the masterpiece called life, own it and master it so that life does not master you.

In this book, I will walk you through the step by step process of how to navigate your way to success as an immigrant in any field of your choosing.

Most immigrants start at the bottom and make their way up. Our paths can be difficult and scary. It may take a while for us to get to where we want to. But remember that you have it within you to make it. You had the courage to face the unknown when you decided to leave what you were familiar with. You traded the support of the people you knew and loved to a place where you may not know anyone, where customs and language were strange to you. It may be a lonely journey but your burning desire to have a better future for yourself and for your loved ones overcomes your personal struggles. I admire you and I cheer you on.

My name is Kathryn and I'm your friend in this journey. As your friend, I would like to introduce myself. I am an immigrant born and raised in the Philippines. At age 24, I came to Canada as a student and later on worked as a pharmacist in Ontario, Canada. My journey had been difficult but not unique. It is shared by many other immigrants trying to make a life in another country. As of the time of writing this book, I have been in my adopted country for fifteen years. I have learned much and have been able to conquer what to me was a seemingly overwhelming odds and financial setbacks. Like many immigrants, I struggled financially, emotionally and physically to get to where I am now. I also struggled with self-doubt, indecision, wrong decisions, wrong ideas about myself and others.
However, I am fortunate and blessed to have mentors guiding and teaching me principles to attain success in different areas in my life. I would like to give you the same opportunity as I was given through this book and hope that this will change your life for the better.

Professionally, I am a practicing pharmacist and also a certified personal development coach. My passion lies in helping people become the best version of themselves and help them grow. I have taught, coached and mentored many immigrants from all kinds of nationalities and backgrounds. I've watched them grow and succeed. I would like to have the opportunity to help many others in their quest for success and fulfilment. This is why I decided to write this book, to reach out to you and many others who are like you and me – immigrants or ones who are working in another country to help and provide for their families.

I want to show you that you can do it! You can have the life that you desire! I too started as an immigrant student with an uncertain future. I became a pharmacist and eventually became a successful leader in my industry. Today, I am a Transformational and Success Coach, a member of the John Maxwell team - the leading leadership company in the world, an author and speaker.

I hope that this book will become your companion and your guide in your success journey. You will learn practical ways to help you in your path to success.

The Challenges of An Immigrant

In 2003, Zellers company sponsored me to come to Canada and granted me a loan while I studied for my Pharmacy equivalency exams. I had major uncertainties about the future. What if I don't pass my exams? How can I repay the money I owed to this company? I owed the company about forty-five thousand dollars for my schooling, exam fees, food and lodging. How would I go about processing my papers to be able to stay in Canada long-term? Would I be successful here? What if I am not successful, how would I live my life then?

Although we learned English in school since grade school, I still had communication problems. I realized that there are different versions of English language and that the words we learned in school are not necessarily the ones people use in conversations. I had to learn to speak casually and conversationally. As a health care professional, I learned that I have to use different words to refer to the same thing when speaking to different audiences.

I faced discrimination and people's mistaken belief that because I am of a different background I somehow knew way less than other people in my profession. Because of these challenges, I resolved to learn everything that I can to be effective in communication, learn strategies to be successful and effectively place them into practice.

As an immigrant, we face a lot of barriers to success. It may be language and communication, cultural barrier, financial barrier, residency status or work status. You can probably think of more things that are standing in our way to success. When we first came to our adopted country there were many things we did not know or understand. If you are someone contemplating on immigrating, it is important to equip yourself with knowledge of where you are going, geography, culture and customs, legal documents needed etc. It is also important to try to look ahead and see what are the potential challenges you may face so you can prepare yourself.

There are several ways to prepare yourself. You can find people who can help introduce you to the ways of the new country. It could be friends, family or acquaintances who are already living in that place and know the culture. If they immigrated to that country, they can also guide you on what to do before you get there and when you get there.

There are plenty of information you can find online through government websites that would give you the necessary details regarding required documentation and step by step process for immigrating. Once you get to the country, you can find local organizations to help you make informed decisions in terms of establishing yourself.

Some organizations hold classes and seminars to help you in different areas such as language classes or how to prepare your resume to help you land a job, finances, computer literacy classes etc. There are immigration companies who may be giving free classes so take advantage of those opportunities. Arm yourself with knowledge to be able to go forward faster.

When I came to Toronto, I knew people who have already started the process of getting licensed in Canada. They served as my guide. They gave me tips on how to pass the exams, helped me prepare and lent me emotional support as I go through the process. Depending on where you are and what is available to you, try to find groups of people who are in the same process as you to lend you support.

Language and Communication

One of the most basic requirements for success which is surprisingly overlooked by some is the ability to communicate and to speak the language of the area you are in. In the beginning, I experienced a number of miscommunication issues. As a student, I lived in a place where there was a mixture of people coming from all over the world. In fact, going to the mall for the first time was quite an experience for me. I literally got dizzy trying to identify which possible countries the people I was seeing in the malls were coming from! I had fun though!

There were some interactions when I had to use gestures to communicate or draw what I needed to communicate since the person I was talking to did not know how to speak English and I did not know how to speak the other person's language. It was very strange at first, but I got used to it.

When I first came to Toronto in 2003, I had an embarrassing situation where I was counselling a patient on one of his medications and I did not know how to translate my pharmacy technical jargon into something easy to understand by someone not familiar with pharmaceutical terms. I was fortunate enough that someone "rescued" the situation by re-interpreting my words and everybody went away happy…well except me.

At that time, I was studying the bridging course for pharmacy with my roommates. We resolved to practice conversational English often that we even spoke English with each other. We just wanted to get good at it!

The company I worked for assigned me to different neighborhoods with differing predominant languages and cultures. As a student, I worked with Chinese population, then East Asian then moved to French-Canadian community. There were frustrations and miscommunications as some are unable to speak English and I don't speak their language either.

If you think about it, even when you are dealing with people who speaks the same language that you do you can still have misunderstandings. How much more when you are dealing with people of different cultural background.

Some who are highly capable and with the right credentials are missing opportunities for work or business because they cannot speak the language. I'd like to encourage you to practice consistently if you are lacking in verbal communication skills.

Talk to locals or native speakers. Listen to the way they speak, the way they use certain words and pay attention to 'slang' words. If you don't understand what those words and phrases mean, politely ask them. Listen closely to the inflection and intonation of the words. The more you can speak like the native speakers the more understandable you become and the easier it is to converse with you and vice-versa.

Verbal communication is an art by itself and it requires practice. There is another language component that holds a lot more weight in terms of conveying the meaning we want to convey. It is our non-verbal communication.

The essence of communication is people understanding each other. Your body language speaks volumes. Consider your cultural differences. Happiness, sadness, disgust, fear, anger and surprise may be shown in different degrees of expression.

Know the most commonly used non-verbal form of communication. For example, in the western world nodding the head means "yes" while in some cultures it means "no". In India, tilting the head side to side means yes. Nodding head up and down in Japan means the person is listening to you.

Eye contact in western culture shows attentiveness and respect but is considered rude and offensive in Asia and Middle East. It is especially offensive when you make eye contact with women as it conveys power or sexual interest. Prolonged eye contact in Asia means you are challenging the other person. In South America, prolonged eye contact by members of opposite sex shows interest, however, when a female makes prolonged eye contact with another female it often means criticism of the other person's appearance.

Forms of touch such as kissing, and hugging are common in western culture. However, in Asia people are more conservative with these gestures. Shaking hands is acceptable in many cultures although the degree of firmness in the handshake differs. Right hand is usually used for handshakes especially in Asia and Middle East. Common understanding dictates that the left hand is reserved for personal hygiene.

Burping in Asia means you really appreciate the food while in the west it is considered rude. Consider also the acceptable personal space in the culture you are in. Conversing in Middle East are usually done in closed proximity while other cultures there is a degree of physical space that is acceptable.

Giggling may mean embarrassment or unease or happiness in Filipino culture and can be misunderstood very easily. Some people may also use indirect communication for example, asking about a family member instead of directly saying 'how are you?'.

Pointing with your lips instead of using words to convey direction is perfectly acceptable in the Philippines but the person you are talking to, if not familiar with it simply would not understand. It may just look like you are grimacing or making a strange facial expression and can be easily misunderstood.

Great communicators know the secret to communicating effectively. You need to be able to create rapport to communicate at a much higher level. Rapport is your ability to be in sync with the person you are speaking to such that you establish ease of communication and exert influence.

Language is both verbal and non-verbal and communication a two-way street. Your ability to give and receive information effectively is a must if you want massive success.

Culture

Coming from a different cultural background we have much to learn from others. The reason for learning the culture is to connect with people. Only when you begin to make connections that your path to success starts. Connections allow you to gain access to resources that otherwise you may not know about or have access to. Connections allow you to become part of a community and be able to settle down and build your life in a foreign country.

When I was assigned by my company to Northern part of Ontario, I realized very quickly that I am out of my depths here, with no friends and no family and no idea what to expect. There needs to be something I must do to improve my situation. I will have to learn their culture to improve my odds of becoming successful in gaining the confidence of the people around me.

I resolved to take the initiative to give to my co-workers in a meaningful way. With intention, I taught the pharmacy assistants I worked with and trained them voluntarily without being told to by my boss. In return, I gained the trust of the people I worked with.

Some became my friends and taught me the Canadians' way of life. They invited me to their homes, so I was able to observe how they interact with each other, with their families and friends. They showed me how to ice-skate and enjoy things like fishing, snowmobiling, tobogganing down a hill in wintertime and watching the stars while being pulled up the hill.

I rented a room with a woman named Fran who at that time was 65 years old and retired. She became my walking and biking buddy. We walked in the woods during summer, spring, fall and winter. Fran would talk to me about the black bears in the area, the raccoons, skunks, rabbits, birds and the many different foliage. I spent the weekends exploring the place and sometimes went to the cottage and fishing with my new-found friends. When we were at Fran's cottage, we would go look for mushrooms and spend time enjoying each other's company.

I was genuinely interested in the people I met, and they were also interested in me. I shared stories of home and how we do things differently and would cook them food from my own country. Sometimes, I would knock on their doors and offer them the food that I made, and we sit together and chat. They would also offer me food and new things to try and do. I would offer to shovel snow and tend their gardens to be able to spend time and learn from them. They made me appreciate the new country I am in.

Make new friends and have them show you their culture and norms. Learning your adopted country's customs and traditions will help you appreciate your new place and the people.

Some cultures are more tolerant and some not so. Be willing to exchange ideas with others and learn the do's and don'ts of their culture.

Financial

Money was tight as a student. I was fortunate to come with a bunch of other students. I remembered when we first came, we learned that people throw stuff away like couches and other furniture. Since we did not have extra money to spend on furniture, for the first few weeks after arriving in Toronto, every day early in the morning before we went to school we would wait in front of the window facing the garbage area in our apartment complex. If something is there, we would then race downstairs and try to be the first one to get to the area to see if the furniture that is sitting there is good enough to use. We would race against our other friends who are also doing the same thing. We gathered a few couches that way and were late to class a few times. The dean of the school was quite upset when we were late until she heard of what we were doing and felt bad for us so we were forgiven for our tardiness. I am proud to say that because my roommates woke up early and were fast, our apartment was one with the most couches, it became a hub for friends from other apartments to gather together.

Finances is truly one of the most challenging things as an immigrant. We have to make sacrifices in order to get financially stable. Some of us have the added pressure of being responsible for the people we left behind in our own home countries.

Many of the immigrants take odd jobs to work towards their future. Rajesh Mehta, an immigrant born and raised in India was a university professor with a master's degree and came from a wealthy family background. When he immigrated to Canada he had to start from the bottom. As he was going through the process of becoming a licensed pharmacist, he worked sewing trousers and sewing shoes. But Rajesh knew who he was and what he was capable of. Rajesh became a proud owner of multiple pharmacies. He currently serves as Senior Director of Marketing in one of the insurance companies in Canada on top of owning his own pharmacy.

In my interview with Rajesh, I asked him what advice he would give to immigrants in order to succeed. He said, "you must be willing to work hard and not mind the jobs you need to do at first, have faith in God, be courageous and keep on hoping."

My husband David, also came from an influential and affluent family. David worked in graphics and animation industry but could not find a job in his field when we moved to Kingston, Ontario. It motivated him to create his own company. To fund his ventures, he needed to take odd jobs like shoveling snow in the mornings or nights in minus 20 plus degree weather. He did landscaping, painting, door to door sales and many more. Oftentimes, when he was doing snow removal I would find my husband shivering from the cold after shoveling snow all night, but he was determined. He came to this country to become successful and he was willing to do any job so he can pursue what he desired.

Be prepared to make sacrifices to go for your dreams. It is also very important to educate yourself in terms of handling finances. Know where to get support if you are a student, how to get loans to start a business or go for further education etc. It is very important to make a plan. Study people who are financially successful and let them serve as your guide to achieve success in this area. Financial planning is essential if you want a future that you want to enjoy.

It is important to learn to create boundaries with your finances especially if you are one of those people who is challenged with being the sole breadwinner in your family. Many immigrants go to another country but with families depending on them for their needs. You need to be able to take care of yourself before you can take care of others. Make sure you have savings for when you need them. If you are alone in that country with no other family, it is crucial because if you get sick and unable to work or if you lose your job, you have no family to go home to and take care of you in the meantime. You may want to get a disability insurance and contribute to employment insurance if available just in case.

For those who have families "back home", I hope that you are not equating money with love. I know some people who have not gone back to their families for 10 or 20 years because they thought money was more important to their families than their presence. It is truly sad when you begin to think of yourself as just a moneymaker for the rest of your family. Go home. Make them feel your love by your presence.

Discrimination

An aggressive voice on the phone can be heard saying," Where are you from?", "Where did you graduate?", "How come you could not read my writing?", you "Paki!!!". This was one of Rajesh' experience of discrimination by a doctor who wrote a prescription in "chicken-scratch" writing prompting him to call the doctor to verify the order. Rajesh has a Bachelor of Pharmacy degree and a master's degree in chemistry, a highly educated individual who studied and speaks in English and a university professor. This was how he was treated by the doctor because his accent gave him away as not from "here".

I stayed in Toronto for a year and a half and because the city is multicultural I did not experience prejudice. When I got my first job however, I was in a place where an Asian healthcare professional is uncommon, I got my taste of discrimination.

People were wary of me. They did not trust me at first. Some would have asked me how I ended up working in pharmacy in a community of French speaking white people and yes, I did face discrimination. Some people did not believe that I hold a degree in pharmacy. Some would even tell me that they heard that in Asia, you can buy diplomas and certificates and asked me if I just bought mine.

There were those who were supposed to be under my supervision who looked down on me and instead of doing their job would command me to do theirs instead. During my first year of working as a pharmacist I toughened up as I realized that no one would stand up for me if I will not stand up for myself and learn the necessary skills to survive and thrive in this new country.

It was a very difficult time of adjustment but the longer I stayed there and the more they got to know me the better my relationship with other people become. As I understood them, and they understood me, my relationships with my patients, co-workers and neighbors got better through time. The more I understood them and the more they understood me, all forms of prejudice and discrimination disappeared.

So how do we deal with discrimination and prejudice? Always give your best. Show up with your best self. Even when you are having a difficult time mentally, emotionally, strive to show up positive at your workplace and smile. A smiling person is an inviting presence and it makes people feel good when you smile at them.

Do your best to get yourself pumped up and ready for work. One thing that helped sustain me was exercising and listening to upbeat music before I go to work so I have stamina and the increased serotonin in my body gave me a good feeling to start my day. When you are feeling good, you show up ready to give. Give people the extra kindness. Prejudice fades with kindness.

Technical Aspects and Documentation

1. Make sure you have proper documents needed to be in that country such as documents needed to legally work or study.

2. If you are planning to stay for good, know the residency process by going to the government websites yourself. Ensure that you are well informed of the required legalities.

3. Know how to transfer your skillset to your current situation. Contact Colleges and Universities if you want to transfer credits from your Degree or Diploma.

4. Know your rights – get informed of your rights. Some immigrants are taken advantage of because they are unaware of their rights.

5. Know the appropriate government agencies that can help you.

6. Organize you need to do and the documents you need to have. For ease of tracking you may use the following format.

Organize your to do list by filling this form:

What I need to do	Documents Needed	When to complete

PART 2

SUCCESS BEGINS WITHIN YOU

Success Begins Within You
– It starts with knowing and understanding your own self

In 1943, Abraham Harold Maslow a psychologist theorized that there are fundamental needs that we humans have. The most basic need for food, water, warmth and rest, and self-actualization as our highest-level need. His theory suggests that the most basic level of needs must be met before the individual will strongly desire and become motivated to go for the secondary or higher-level needs. It means that as humans we only begin to think of following our true heart's desire to develop ourselves to our full potential once we have food, water, warmth, rest and that we feel safe and that we have a sense of belongingness and that we achieved a certain level of accomplishment.

As an immigrant, I watched myself go through the whole process of meeting my own needs and that of my family "back home" to accomplishment and then to self-actualization. Meaning I get to live my dream life! Some of us who came from third world countries know very well the struggles of having to provide for the basic needs of the family where there is no social assistance or even a credit card to use "just in case I get into bad times".

I don't know about you, but in my case, I was "sent" to Canada to support my family so for a long time that is what I did. I was blessed to have a good job that paid well and as I developed relationships and grew in my skill sets I had begun to dream of becoming "more".

An immigrant's journey to success is a tough one because we were taught to live for our families without regard to "self". Many of my fellow countrymen go to other countries to earn money and send everything to their families. Many hold multiple jobs to support themselves and their families.
In our striving to provide for our families, we forget that we also matter.

In this book, I will help you become successful and fulfilled. It may take a while but as long as you follow the principles stated in this book you will surely meet success along the way.

Your Money Mindset Driver

How you view money affects your personal finance and financial success. I came from a background where poverty was the norm. My upbringing made me unconsciously view people who had money as someone who are greedy and selfish people. As a consequence, even though I started earning a lot of money, I squandered money away as if there was no tomorrow out of guilt and thus sabotaged my financial success.

I stayed in that poor mentality and poor attitude for years until I realized the foolishness of my actions. I decided I needed to change and to change my mindset I needed help. I hired a coach specifically to help me in this area of my life and for a year worked on my mindset and attitude. It has made a difference in my life. Money is the currency for which we trade our skills, abilities and time for. Money enables us to get the material things that we desire and provide for our needs and that of our family. It is important therefore for us, you and I to spend time together in this matter in this section of the book. It is important that we have the right attitude about money and the creation of wealth.

You probably heard it when people say that money is the root of all evil and looks at the accumulation of money as if it is dirty or immoral. The truth is it is neither good or evil. If you are a person of good character, you will use that money for good. If you are a person of bad character, you may use that money to do harmful things to you or to others. Money is simply a transactional tool. It is used as an exchange for the service we perform for someone whether it was an exchange for goods or for services. Therefore, money is good when achieved honestly through ones' abilities and skills.

Economy runs by an exchange of goods and services. The greater the amount or the better quality of goods or service you render and the level of difficulty and the difficulty of accessing the goods or service determines its value. For example, specialists are paid more than general practitioners, labor jobs vary in value of service rendered depending on the complexity and specialized knowledge required. A product that is hard to acquire cost more than a product that is readily available.

When choosing a career or a job or if you want to run a successful business, consider these principles of economics. Decide what quality of financial life you want to live and consider the factors that would give you favorable economic result.

Money increases in proportion to the number of people you serve and of the difficulty of the job. For example, if as an employee you serve mostly yourself and your boss, you will be paid a certain amount of wage. If you decide to serve others such as your coworkers, you will be seen as someone reliable and trustworthy and your boss may decide to increase your wage. When you learn the skillset to lead others you become more valuable to your boss and may get yet another increase. As your expertise grow, your compensation grows.

Business owners risk their own money to build a business and employ people. They serve the customers and by employing people they serve those employees extending that service to their employees' family. In return, they receive a much bigger portion as compensation.

It is in the service of others that we benefit. This is a give and take world that we live. We are all interconnected in this way. The more people you help, the more you get compensated for your time and effort. Give more than you expect to receive.

To Be Hugely Successful You Must Know Yourself

My mentors are successful entrepreneurs. Some of them millionaires and they tell me that I am no less than them. That surprised and challenged me because I did not view myself that way. Successful people think differently. They do not do what most of us are content to do. If I want to be successful as they are I need to learn to think differently.

The purpose of this chapter is for you to realize that you have a major role in how you experience life, to not treat yourself as a victim of circumstances. I hope that after reading this chapter, your awareness of your own self increases, and you will realize the potential you have within you.

Although the easiest thing in the world is to be ourselves and the most difficult thing in the world is to be what other people want us to be, we are still very much influenced by what "people" think about what we should do. To know yourself you need to give yourself permission to go where your interests truly lies.

The journey may be long and may take many turns. I came to Canada as a student then became a pharmacist, however, I was less than satisfied with my career and contemplated on pursuing a medical degree. I studied and took review classes went through the whole process of examination and contacting the university to study medicine.

Before enrolment to a medical school, I realized that I was only doing it because it was ingrained in my culture that to be successful one choice is to be a doctor so I did not go through with it as originally intended. I studied interior design instead and got certified in interior design as well as studied real estate investing. I did all these while at the same time having a full-time pharmacist job. When I say I studied, I really did immerse myself in the subject. I even went to networking events and seminars. I also did some other entrepreneurial ventures. In this process of trying new things I learned something about myself. There was something missing in what I was doing. Although I had the initial interest, I was unsuccessful in these ventures simply because I lacked the necessary passion to continue to pursue them.

In all those years of trying different ventures and studying different things, there was one consistent area that stood out. I was very passionate about it that I would do it for free all the time but never thought of it as something I could make money from. I loved coaching, training, developing and equipping people! I loved helping people grow to their maximum potential. It is when I am doing these things that my heart soars and my best self shows up.

My interest in the field of personal development started in 2010 at the point in my life when I felt stuck. I was frustrated because I knew there was more to me than what is showing up in my life. After speaking to a coach and seeking confirmation from different people who knew me, I decided to become a Certified Coach, Speaker and Facilitator with the John Maxwell Team. JMT is currently the leading leadership company in the world spearheading transformational work in countries all over the world through value-based leadership principles. I studied psychology of success, Neurolinguistic Programming (NLP) which is the field of study of the brain both conscious and subconscious and how it can be programmed for success.

It took a while for me to get to know who I am and what I wanted in my life. When I started telling people that what I want to do is to develop others, some of them gave me encouragement while some are doubtful if I would make it a reality.

The thing is you are the only one who truly knows yourself and knows your capability deep down inside. Go for your dreams even if the rest of the world tells you otherwise. I would like to encourage you that while you are out there making a living, gradually steer yourself to where you truly want to go.

Know Yourself - Dreams and Aspirations

"You can't imprison greatness. You can't lock away a dream."
– John C. Maxwell

To dare to dream was to live in fear of being labelled as selfish. But I dared to dream....

I've been there. I wanted to do something else and become something else other than what I am supposed to be. What I was capable of and how I saw myself was hugely dependent on how my family "saw" me. I wanted to grow but, in my mind, it was impossible because I was expected to take care of my family and other people who were looking up to my family for help. I thought I only existed for that purpose. I felt that I did not have a right to go after my dreams but was expected to fulfill other people's dreams. What I thought was probably untrue but that was how I saw it and that was my reality.

Oftentimes though we make this as an excuse not to go after our dreams when the truth is we are scared to go for our dreams, scared to fail. The funny thing is we would do whatever our family or other people dreamed for us even though it is hard. We struggle emotionally because that is not what we want in the first place. We also struggle because they may not be our strengths. We are not functioning using our strengths, but we do it anyway.

It is strange how our minds work to trick us into believing that we cannot do something just because somebody else expects us to be something else. I suspect that the real reason we do this is we equate love with suppressing who we truly are to please "them". Another thing that comes to mind which is truer for me than the other is, I was just scared. Too scared to follow my dreams unless I fail. At least if those were other people's dreams for me, I could at least blame "them" if I fail.

Now let's talk about you and your dreams. What is it for you? What are your hidden reasons for not following your dreams? It is time you too to get out of that mindset, having your own dreams is not selfish. In fact, when you truly live your dream you will be happier and whatever blessings come your way you are more willing to give not out of obligation but because of the joy it brings you to see them happy too.

Erwin McManus in his TEDx talk, said that "Humans as a species has a unique characteristic. We are the only species who can materialize the invisible in the future. We are creativity wrapped up in skin.... our imagination is both a gift and a curse. We imagine ideals and create the cause of those ideals and we also imagine who we are not and the life we are experiencing and the world we are not creating, and we become unhappy. As humans, we are driven by the invisible and that invisible world within us is translated into the external. We create who we are. We imagine, and we create."[1]

You are indeed a unique human being with a glorious future you cannot even begin to imagine unless you engage this precious ability within you to dream, to create from your imagination. Starting now, begin to engage and dream for your future.

Now that we establish that you are a creative being, let us step into a different realm of existence for you. At this point, I will lead you to begin your creative journey.

Make yourself comfortable, take a deep breath and begin to imagine yourself 5 years from now and 10 years from now.

Write your vision on this page:

I encourage you to take a moment and reflect on where you are right now. As you ponder these questions write them on a journal, you will find that a lot of things will go through your mind. There will be voices in your head telling you this is what you want, no "this one" or "that one". It may get confusing at first that is why I tell you to write everything down.

Be patient with yourself. It may not come right away, it could take months for you to find out what it is that you truly desire but the important thing is that now you are beginning to think about your own dreams. Look back on the thoughts you wrote in your journal, find the common thread and you will find what it is that you truly desire.

You have found it when you can imagine a future that energizes your mind, will and emotions, one that empowers you to do everything you can to achieve it.

Reflection time: Ask yourself the following questions and write down your answers.

Is my life my dream life? If not why?

_____

_____

_____

_____

_____

_____

_____

_____

_____

_____

_____

_____

Are my dreams, mine or were these other people's dreams for me? Am I living my family's dreams for me? Were they my parents' dreams for me?

_____

_____

_____

_____

_____

_____

_____

What do I truly desire?

_____

_____

_____

_____

_____

_____

Describe what you envisioned in detail:

I want to be:

_____

_____

_____

_____

_____

_____

_____

I want to do:

_____

_____

_____

_____

_____

_____

What do I like?

_____

_____

_____

_____

_____

_____

What would make me feel really good?

_____

_____

_____

_____

_____

_____

_____

What would I love to do?

What would I love to be?

For some it is easier to draw what they want. You may draw a picture of your highest aspiration here.

Know Yourself - Passion

Highly successful people are passionate about what they do. Your passion is your fuel. Love what you do. The way you know that you are passionate about something is that you are willing to do the thing even though you are not paid for it. Keep the desire burning by surrounding yourself with like-minded people.

I often enjoy artists on stage giving their all. They capture the audience attention with the passion they display. It is magnetic and riveting to watch. Perhaps part of my fascination is that I wish and hope to be like them – fearless, skillful and filled with passion.

When you are passionate, it naturally moves people. It draws people to you. There is something about passionate people that attracts others and makes people like them. They make others feel alive. They make others feel engaged.

For some, knowing what they are passionate about is easy but for some people, it takes intentional discovery to know their passion. Knowing what you are truly passionate about is a process and may take time. Be patient with yourself if at the moment you do not know what it is.

One way you can tell is if the thing you want to do you are still willing to do even for free. Also, with whatever it is you are doing even if it takes hours to do and you still willingly do it without anybody telling you to do so, chances are you are doing what you are passionate about.

They say passion is a feeling of 'burning desire' for something. It is easy to mistake excitement for something 'new' as passion. Many times, I had a 'burning desire' to achieve something that I mistook for passion. It was instead a 'burning desire' to win or to achieve a particular 'title' to be added to my name, a certification or another notch to my achievements. If you are an achiever, you may fall into this trap.

So how do you determine if you are passionate about something? Notice that throughout your life, there are times when you are doing something, and you are totally involved in whatever you are doing, without awareness to time or even the people around you. You are totally focused and when you are in that moment, you feel a sense of calm and completeness. It seems that nothing matters except whatever you are doing. You also feel joy that you cannot explain. It is just 'there'.

Notice and record those times, they will point you to the direction of your passion.

If you want to find out what your passion is, take time to notice what are you naturally drawn to. Remember the times in your life when you felt like nothing else exist other than what you are doing.

The Passion Process

Write what you are doing and ask yourself the following questions when engaging in something or doing a task:

How do I feel in my body?

_____

Does my heart skip a beat?

_____

Do I feel like I'm in the zone?

_____

Do I find it thrilling?

_____

Does it inspire me to be better even without other people telling me to?

_____

Does it give me energy?

_____

Know Your Why – Your Purpose

"Life depends on you and your choices. The real value of your life largely depends on what you do with your life. You either move the world or the world moves you! You were born to either show the world why you were born or the world shows you why you were born, period!"
— *Ernest Agyemang Yeboah*

Life is more than about financial success. It is about purpose. What is purpose? Purpose is having a sense of doing something greater than yourself that when you've achieved it, you will feel that your life is worth living. Viktor E. Frankl was a psychiatrist who survived the Nazi concentration camp. He lost everything he had, his family and friends. He experienced intolerable suffering. Later on he recalled in his book "Man's Search for Meaning" that the one thing that kept him going was the book he was going to write detailing his experiences. Humankind can endure greater sufferings when they have a sense of purpose.

People who feel like they have a purpose are willing to do more and give more. They are willing to endure more because they are driven by their purpose. They are less likely to suffer depression when things do not go their way or when the picture they have of their life does not match their current reality. They cling to hope. They carry themselves differently and they present themselves to the world differently.

I see it in my parents, they have big dreams to help the people in their community. When Typhoon Haiyan hit the island of Leyte in Philippines, thousands of people died and thousands more lost their homes and livelihood. My parents helped rebuild the community. They were willing to suffer the losses and shoulder the burdens of caring for people because they felt called to uplift the conditions of the community they were in. Although they are in their sixties they worked very hard for their vision, providing hope and livelihood to the people.

When we do not have a purpose, we might be working and making money but short on fulfillment. We get drained and tired and eventually get disillusioned with life. I urge you to find your purpose so that at the end of your life you can say to yourself, it is worth it, and I've lived a satisfying life.

Purpose is what gives life meaning. It gives us strength when we go through life's difficulties.

Know Yourself - Self-Awareness

> *"Know your enemy and yourself, and in one thousand battles you will never be in peril. When you are ignorant of the enemy but know yourself, your chances of winning or losing are equal. If ignorant both of your enemy and of yourself, you are certain, in every battle, to be in peril."*
> *-Sun Tsu, The Art of War*

March to your own beat, sing to your own tune, it means show up to the world with your authentic self.

Who are you on the inside?

You must understand yourself to be truly successful, Successful people understand their strengths and weaknesses. They focus on doing what they are good at but continually push themselves out of their comfort zone.

Reflection time: Ask yourself the following questions.

What makes me sad?

_____

_____

_____

_____

_____

_____

What give me true joy? (happiness vs joy)

_____

_____

_____

_____

_____

_____

What drives me to do what I do?

_____

_____

_____

_____

_____

_____

What are my existing skill sets?

_____

_____

_____

_____

_____

What am I good at? How can I make it better?

_____

_____

_____

_____

_____

_____

Know Yourself – Beliefs

"Until you make the unconscious conscious, it will direct your life and you will call it fate. "
- Carl Jung

Beliefs are ideas that we believe to be true and the types of beliefs that affect our behavior are those that we believe to be true about ourselves. Beliefs are very powerful in shaping our behaviors. The beliefs we hold about ourselves, about others and the world around us drive our behavior. It influences our perception of the world and events around us. We interpret events through the lens of our beliefs.

Our behavior determines our reality which can then affect whether we become successful or not. It is important to understand how we come to believe and know what we believe about ourselves, about others and about our circumstances. Beliefs are formed in different ways. It is formed when an idea is repeated over and over again until it is fixed in our nonconscious mind and it becomes a habit. Belief is also formed when something happens to us that affects us emotionally and forms our belief.[2,3]

"As a man thinketh in his heart so is he." Proverbs 23:7. What we constantly think about creates a permanent pattern that becomes our belief. Our belief about ourselves informs the results that we get in life. If there is an outcome you want in your life and is not showing up, examine the beliefs you have about yourself. You may be unknowingly sabotaging yourself.

For example, I've learned a long time ago that comparing myself with others only makes me miserable, so I resolved to only compare myself with my own self and as long as I am improving I am happy and content. If I believe that I am less than capable then I would not even try to do something where I already think I would fail. Whatever it is I believe about myself, I become it.

Most of us think that the thoughts we think are ours. Do you know that most people actually do not think? Most people only regurgitate or replay information based on what they were told by social media, their peers, co-workers etc. and have opinions based on the popular opinion at that time.

We are being manipulated day after day to make us to go a certain way, think certain thoughts, do things, buy stuff etc. Media and culture influence and shape peoples' beliefs about themselves. Be careful with what you let yourself believe in. Examine and ask questions why.

A book Quantum: A Guide to the Perplexed by Al Khalili discussed what physicists called the Observer Effect. The Observer Effect is the phenomenon in the quantum world that happens when someone 'looks' to take a measurement of an electron, it is the act of measurement itself that causes electrons to be limited to a single possibility (either a particle or a wave).[4] This makes for an interesting question, "How does the electron intuitively know that is being observed?" This discovery led me to think that if the electrons in an atom behave in a certain way depending on whether they are observed or not, and if our physical bodies are made up of atoms, is it possible that the way we see or think of ourselves will determine who we are going to become? I believe this is true in our human world.

Are you aware that your thoughts build your "reality"? James Allen said, "In life we will never get what we want, we get what we believe we are capable of achieving" We don't get what we want, we get who we are.

For example, if I believed myself to be incapable or writing this book I will never write this book or any book at all in my life even though I truly desire to write a book.

Look at the results you had so far and examine the way you see yourself.

Know Yourself - Let Go of Things that Hold You Back

Our thoughts mold us. Indeed, we become what we think about. Scientists have discovered that thoughts are real physical things in our brain. Dr. Caroline Leaf, neuroscientist explains the concept of our ability to change ourselves through thinking thoroughly in her book "Switch on Your Brain, The Key to Peak Happiness, Thinking, and Health"

Dr. Leaf's research into brain plasticity showed that we as human beings have this amazing ability to be able to change our brain structure moment by moment, day by day through our thinking.

The act of thinking lead to the creation of protein structures in our brains that houses the thought. Every thought has emotions attached to it. The amazing thing is that you have the power and ability to redirect your thinking to be more resourceful, purposeful and creative. We can consciously direct our thinking. This is how we can take out damaging patterns of thinking and replace them with healthy thoughts. [5]

There is an internal self-image that we hold and that self-image dictates what we believe. That self-image could be your friend or your enemy. It will set up expectations such that whenever there is an opportunity for us to do something beyond what we are used to, the conditions and circumstances and the comfort zone we have at that time, we will believe that we are incapable of doing it. This is why most people stay the way they are. When we stay this way and not allow ourselves to change believing that we are who we will always be and unable to change, we have already set ourselves up for failure in our self-limiting belief.

Self-limiting beliefs are beliefs that we place on us that limits us. For example, saying to yourself "I cannot learn anything new", "I am too old to learn new things", "I am not skilled enough". Negative self-judgement such as saying to yourself "I am dumb and stupid", "I am not tall enough" or "I am not pretty enough, "I do not have enough education", or "I don't have enough money" sets you up for failure. Self-limiting beliefs and negative self-judgement serve as blocks towards us fulfilling our dreams and aspirations.

Eliminate the distractions of negative thinking. The way you talk to yourself or think of things becomes the ceiling of your potential. We cannot go beyond what we tell ourselves we can. Therefore, you must make every effort to eliminate all negative self-talk.

We must ask ourselves where did they come from? They are the voices in your life that have been conditioned into your subconscious. Most of the beliefs you formed have been programmed into you before the age of reason, before you had the ability to reason and think for yourself. When we are young we have misguided reasoning that is stored in our memory. A young child's capacity to reason and evaluate is not fully developed. A child cannot ascertain the intent of what was said but only registers the emotion.

These beliefs are beliefs that you absorbed from your surroundings. They could have come from your family, they could have come from your parents or other children when you were growing up. It could also be ingrained in your culture. They are emotional imprints that you have attached meaning to regardless of whether they are true or not, have taken root and stayed beyond the realm of your conscious mind.

Self-judgement is one of the major causes of fear, anxiety, anger, depression, hopelessness and inaction. Yet most people don't realize that these feelings are caused by the way they think and speak about themselves. It is caused by their own negative self-talk and when you lack awareness you blame other people. Some of us live with a degree of self-punishment for our negative self-judgement.

A person who constantly think of negative thoughts would have attitudes that are mostly negative towards themselves and others. If we constantly think of failure, we will feel like we are a failure and then our lives become a reflection of the failure that we think we are. Negative self-judgement: this is one of the most damaging habit to our spirit.

Whenever we do something new the negative chatter in our thoughts turn up in volume and their frequency increase greatly. "I'm never going to be anywhere at this rate"; "Look how so and so is doing"; "I can't believe I said that"; "I don't think I can do that".

Let me tell you of my own struggle with self-limiting beliefs. During the first year of working as pharmacist in Canada, there were times I would come back to my place crying because it was just too difficult for me. I faced discrimination. There was a cultural, social, and a deeply ingrained Filipino mindset that we are not as good as "white people" as we used to call Westerners.

Our inferiority towards white people was part of our self-identity as a nation. This negative self-judgement was inflicted in my spirit, took root and became one of the dominant self-image that I used to hold about myself.

Another narrative I used to tell myself was "I am too short; how will people ever listen to me and respect me". Somehow, I equated being tall as being a better specimen of a human being. With these negative self-judgements, I did not go for what I wanted such as going for a higher position in my company for fear of being perceived as not enough.

Self-judgements are very effective in hurting us at our core spiritual level. It gives us self-doubt, it stops possible solutions from developing, it diminishes and marginalizes the vision of what could be. It keeps many people on the realm of what they have already learned, never taking risks.

Yet deep inside they are yearning for more. When I talk to people about their dreams I can see the frustrations and the unbelief they place on themselves. I can see their potential but they remain frozen in their actions because of negative self-judgements.

Operating in an atmosphere of negative self-judgement and criticism deprives us of a large portion of our creativity. It prevents us from deeply connecting to the true essence of who we are. Who we truly are is a deep well of potential waiting to be discovered. When we stay in a zone of self-judgement, we are limited in our access to the resources that God has bestowed upon us.

I urge you to make it your personal mission to destroy limiting beliefs and negative self-judgements that are holding you back from the life you want to live.

We may wonder why we judge ourselves negatively? Interestingly, one of the reasons why we judge ourselves is hope. Think about it for a moment. We hope that self-judgement will protect us from rejection and failure in the eyes of other people.

This may be the reason why for some it can be difficult to overcome. It stems from that false belief that, "If I can judge myself then others will not judge me or reject me. I can be safe from others' hurt if I punish myself first." Somehow when we verbalize our negative self-judgement to others it is in hopes that others would be more forgiving of us. This way we would then feel safe, loved and accepted by them.

We also may have used negative self-judgement to succeed at one time in our lives. This comes from the false belief that, "If I affirm what is worst about me then the pain that it causes would make me do the things I should be doing".

The problem with this kind of thinking is that it tends to scare and immobilize us and we will be unable to take action in the direction of our goals. Our lack of action then creates more anxiety, then more immobilization and it becomes a cycle and before you know it you are completely stuck.

Reflection time: You are responsible for creating your own healthy mind. Healthy mind brings healthy relationships and healthier physical being.

What kinds of thoughts go through your head? Write the thoughts that run constantly through your head.

_____

_____

_____

_____

_____

_____

_____

_____

_____

What is the quality of your thinking? Are they mostly positive or are they mostly negative?

_____

_____

_____

_____

_____

_____

_____

_____

_____

_____

List your self-limiting beliefs:

_____

_____

_____

_____

_____

_____

_____

_____

_____

Negative self-judgement is a form of hatred that is directed to yourself. If you can name it, then you can take massive leaps to freedom.

Write your negative self-judgements (e.g. I am not good enough, pretty enough, powerful enough etc.). What are your projected negative self-judgement in people? We project judgement to others based on who we are.

_____

_____

_____

_____

_____

_____

_____

_____

_____

What are the conditions you put on yourself to accept yourself? (e.g. if I am smart enough, attractive enough, if I have more money, more charm, healthy enough etc.) Attaching conditions to our own life makes us compare ourselves to others to see if we measure up. Reflect on the possible reasons why you are thinking those thoughts without self-judgement. Simply observe your thinking and write your observations.

_____

_____

_____

_____

_____

_____

_____

_____

_____

What do you replace these thoughts with? List ways of how you can improve the quality of your thoughts.

_____

_____

_____

_____

_____

_____

_____

_____

_____

_____

Challenge your current beliefs. Exercise your ability to change your reality by replacing one negative thought to a positive one. Develop a habit of self-acceptance. Repeat daily and as often as you can.

_____

_____

_____

_____

_____

_____

_____

_____

_____

_____

Know How to Market Yourself

"Success is the progressive realization of a worthy idea or goal."
- Earl Nightingale

You may not think about this but we are always broadcasting to the world who we are by the words that we say and the actions that we do. For the world to notice you and help you get to where you want, do what makes you stand out. The best way to market yourself is to show results. Results speak for itself.

Show genuine concern for the things your boss or the company you are working for "care" about. Have a sense of what the leaders you are reporting to care about. Leaders like people who care about their vision and who can bring their vision forward. Know what is important to the company you work for and strive to make significant positive contributions to catch the eye of the important people who can give you a leverage up. For the past couple of years, I have been mentoring someone because I saw her potential and willingness to learn. I gave her projects to give her opportunities to showcase what she can do and for every project that I gave her, her skillsets grew and her confidence grew. Recently, I sat in a meeting with the Vice-President of the company discussing about the vision of where she is taking the company and she asked me who I would recommend for a certain position. Without reservations, I gave the name of this person I am mentoring and the reasons why I recommended her.

Understand what makes you unique. Be bold and show your individuality. Be confident but not arrogant. This is how you will stand out from the rest of the crowd. Do not forget to be open to inputs. In fact, seek input constantly from others you trust, your boss or your peers.

Project confidence and you will feel more confident. Knowing how to "market" yourself to the decision-makers in the company is a good skill to have.

Prepare a short description about what you can do and make it engaging. For instance, I "market" myself as a "growth catalyst" having the gift of being able to create order from chaotic environment, to make sense of what is working and what is not working in terms of processes in an organization. I can see what is good, improve on what works and change the rest. This ability has helped me become a valuable contributor to the companies I worked with and has helped the companies I led grow. I don't necessarily use all those words at the same time, but I use them strategically to let my superiors know this is what I can do for them.

When you go to interviews or when you are networking, having what they call your 'elevator speech' helps people to remember you. The 'elevator speech' is basically your short introduction of who you are and what you do. Create a memorable picture in your audience minds and make your words engaging so that they will remember you.

Be friendly, smile often and greet people with their names. People love it when you use their names in conversations. Be generous with your praise to your co-workers, catch them when they are doing something good and praise them for it. This way people will speak highly of you and perhaps one of those who hears it will open doors for you.

PART 3
THE SUCCESS PROCESS

Success Principles

Achieving success is a process. It does not happen overnight. It requires hard work and discipline. The world is full of eople who have achieved extraordinary success. Their stories are filled with ups and downs, triumphs and tragedies or failures. Let it not dishearten you but let it give you hope that you too will have the success that you want. All you need to do is follow in their footsteps and learn from them.

What I am aiming to do is give you keys to get ahead in your career, job or business. Many people long for success but never really took the time to know and understand the underlying principles that lead to success. Many rely on luck hoping that one day the wheels of fortune will turn their way.

To help you in a practical and effective way I will walk you through establishing a Success Process that you can use for any endeavor you chose to do. Once you have mastered the Success Process you will be able to apply this to any area of your life and watch yourself transform right before your very eyes.

Success Process #1: You Need to Know What You Want. Make Plans and Keep It Simple Enough That It Is Achievable.

Goal Setting

"Make no little plans; they have no magic to stir men's blood….. Make big plans; aim high in hope and world."
– Daniel Hudson Burnham

Ask yourself, "What goal am I trading my life for?". Setting a goal that you know how to do will not give you inspiration.

One of my all-time favorite mentors is Paul Martinelli, President of John Maxwell Team. He shared his wisdom on goal setting. Paul has built multimillion dollar businesses of not just one but multiple businesses including the John Maxwell team. In one of the team, mentorship calls he said: "If you spent more than an hour on planning, you already failed - you are basing your plans based on the conditions and circumstances you know - things never stay the same. If all our time, energy and passion go to the planning stage you become so attached and fall in love with the plan that if things don't fall into plan you will lower your standards to fit your plan." Paul said that sometimes when setting goals, we question whether we are worthy of the goal instead of, 'Is this goal worthy of me?'. He added, you see, if you and I do not have good self-esteem, we will lower our goal to meet the low opinion we hold of ourselves".

His words truly struck a cord within me. I still find myself grasping the meaning of his words and still finds myself questioning if I am worthy of the goal I set for myself. Most especially when my goals seem to be too big and too difficult.

Goals give us clarity. It gives us direction. Set daily goals and long-range goals. Goals must be specific. The more specific you are, the more likelihood you have of achieving it. One tip given by the most successful people in the world is to write your major goal every single day so that it becomes part of your subconscious. Once embedded in your subconscious, it will drive your behavior and subsequently your results.

For goal setting, ask yourself the following questions:

What do I need to do?

_____

What do I need to learn?

_____

Who do I need?

_____

Set dates of completion.

_____

Finally, act quickly and avoid procrastination.

Define What Success Means to You

Personal

Describe what personal success means to you:

Career

Describe what career success means to you:

Family

> **Describe what success for your family means to you:**

Health

> **Describe the best physical/emotional/mental state you want to be in:**

Finances

Describe what financial success look like to you:

Spirituality

Describe the best spiritual state you want to be in:

List the things you want to accomplish in this lifetime:

_____

_____

_____

_____

_____

_____

_____

_____

_____

_____

Knowing why you want to achieve what you want to achieve gets you focused on the goal even when it is difficult. What are the things that are important to you?

_____

_____

_____

_____

_____

_____

_____

_____

_____

Ask yourself what are the things that will stand in my way of reaching my goals?

_____

_____

_____

_____

_____

_____

_____

_____

_____

What is it going to cost you if at some point you decide to give up on your goal?

_____

_____

_____

_____

_____

_____

_____

_____

_____

_____

Success Process #2: Take Action to Get You Closer to Your Desired Result

Once you decided on a course of action act fast. Highly successful people make decisions quickly and take action right away. Procrastination kills momentum. You may take big steps or little steps, it does not matter. Even if you only decide to take 15 minutes out of your day to get to your goal, you are still making progress.

What are your goals?	When would you like it accomplished?	What do you need to do or have to get it done?	Date of completion

Success Process #3: What Are Your results? Analyse and Create Strategies to Maximize Result

You took action, now what? Anytime you invested in reaching a goal, you need to be looking at the results you are getting. In this world, there is a law of nature that is operating at all times, the law of cause and effect. It simply means that for every effect (result), there is a cause. There is a reason for that something to happen or not to happen.

Everything that you do matters in relation to the outcome you want out of your life. If the result that you are getting is favorable, continue to do what you are doing. Be willing to change your behavior or your action if you are not getting the result that you want.

Keep yourself in execution mode, be busy and effective.

Your process needs to look like this. State what you want, then take action. Look at the result and analyze. Ask yourself, "Is this what I want?" If yes, continue; if no, change your action to change the result.

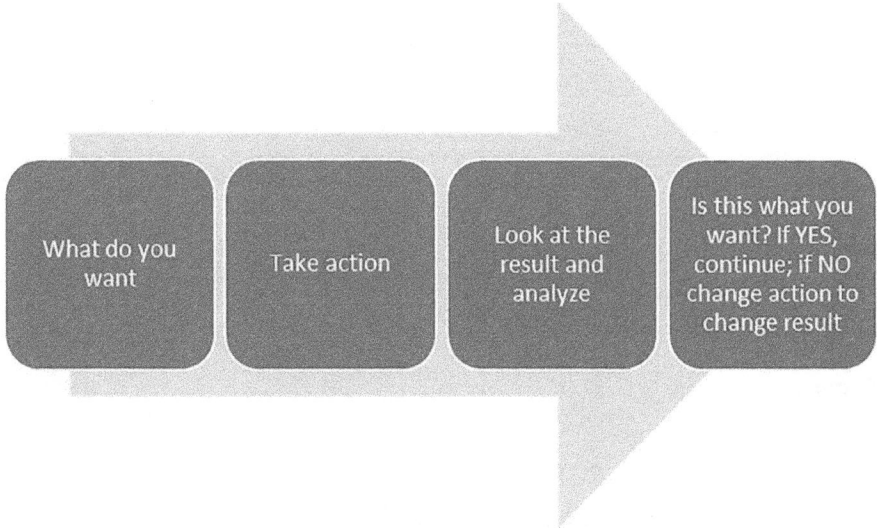

What do you want → Take action → Look at the result and analyze → Is this what you want? If YES, continue; if NO change action to change result

Successful people think differently. They developed a habit of looking for opportunities and acting on those opportunities quickly. If you want to be successful you need to be looking at opportunities and strategies that can help you get to your goal. Keep an open mind to whatever comes your way and see if they would help you get to where you want to go.

Success Process #4: To Get to Where You Want to Go, Be Willing to Change Your Behaviour

Like a ship navigating the seas, be willing to course correct if you go off course. Be willing to change. Read books and articles that can help equip you. The more you read good sources of information the more you learn, the more you learn the more you are able to make decisions quickly.

Practice making decisions. Start with small ones to develop confidence in your ability to take the correct decision. Agility in your thinking give you the advantage. You will make quicker decisions and process information and faster.

Reflection Time: State your goal

_____

Where are you at in relation to your goal in:

2 months

_____

3 months

_____

6 months

_____

1 year

_____

What do you need to change to get the result that you want?

_____

State another goal:

_____

Where are you at in relation to your goal in:

2 months

_____

3 months

_____

6 months

_____

1 year

_____

What do you need to change to get the result that you want?

_____

Success Process #5: Focus on Personal Excellence

Personal Excellence

Personal excellence is being better today than yesterday. One of the people I know who consistently exhibits this trait is George Ho, my former boss. Prior to us working for the same company, he was a director of a long-term care facility and director of a hospital pharmacy before that. He held top positions in organizations he worked for. There is one thing among others that allowed George to stay on top of his field. He insisted on excellence and expected it of himself and of his staff. A person of dedication, he can be seen working way until after everybody had gone home because he wanted to deliver great results for the company. We suspected that his favorite time of the year was during performance reviews. Why? It is because this is an opportunity for him to coach and mentor people individually for them to grow and to be able to give their best in the next few months. He would often be heard saying, "I just need 30 minutes of your time guys!", then 2 hours later you are still talking. Those were the most memorable and productive talks I personally had with any of my bosses. George was greatly admired and loved by his staff because he took time to groom his staff for excellence. His efforts were noted by the company we worked with that when it was time for promotion he quickly rose to the top.

Consistently go above and beyond expectations. Be so good that people have no choice but to acknowledge you for your contribution. The world will eventually compensate you for what you do. John Maxwell teaches it this way, "give maximum value to the people and the organization you work for and specialize, specialize, specialize until you are special."

You have the power and resources within you to make a difference in your life and the lives of others. When you chose to be average, you are depriving yourself and others of the gift of you.

Personally, I invest time and money into developing myself intellectually, mentally, emotionally and spiritually because it is only when we are constantly growing that a bright future is guaranteed. I am happy to say that my husband is also taking a keen interest in developing himself as well and he shares with me what he is learning. He has never been more optimistic than when he is learning and developing himself.

The world will always need those who can be relied to develop the solutions that people are looking for. If you are not growing and improving, there will come a time when you have nothing more to give and when your skillset is no longer relevant the future can look bleak and hopeless. I've seen it happen to one of the best employees in the company I work with. She was the best until new technology came along and she was unwilling to change her negative attitude towards adapting the new technology. Suddenly, the company has no need for her. She went from becoming essential to the company to becoming a liability.

Without growth, you will continue to be where you are in all aspects of your life. If you want to have a better life, then invest in personal development. Take courses, read books, listen to podcasts and webinars, get a mentor/mentors in your industry to help you become better at your craft. If money is an issue, there are free courses you can take that are offered via the internet. There are also courses that are offered for a minimum fee. Go to your local public library, they may have free courses they are offering.

Below are some examples of sites offering courses for free or at minimum fee (note the list is not comprehensive):
www.udemy.com
www.lynda.com
www.coursera.org

Your Personal Excellence Tracker

Hugely successful individuals make a habit of evaluating what they've done and make a concentrated effort to improve it. Follow their footsteps, evaluate your day and see what you can do to improve tomorrow.

What did I do today? What project did I work on?	How can I make it better?

PART 4
PERSONAL POWER

Force Multipliers: Your Personal Power Arsenal

To propel yourself to success, you must develop and use tools to increase your odds. Military science teaches the concept of force multiplications. A **Force Multiplier** refers to a factor or a combination of factors that dramatically increases (hence "multiplies") the effectiveness of an item or group, giving a given number of troops (or other personnel) or weapons (or other hardware) the ability to accomplish greater things than without it.[6]

Force Multipliers are tools that help you multiply, amplify, enlarge or expand your effort to produce more result. Investing in Force Multipliers means that you'll get more done with the same amount of effort.

Force multiplier 1: Knowledge and Skills

Knowledge is the single most valuable currency you own. Your ability to apply that knowledge makes you valuable in any given field. In a competitive environment, you must distinguish yourself. Strive to be known for something. Although, none of us can be good at everything, be the best at something. Find the most valuable knowledge in your industry that can give you an edge, take this one subject and major in it. Immerse yourself on the subject for a month, three months or a year. Keep abreast of the latest innovations in your industry.

Take note that whatever current knowledge you have are fast becoming obsolete. If you want to stay ahead of the game, you must keep replenishing your storehouses of knowledge. Certifications and continuing education programs are a great way to help you stay current and relevant in your field. To have a competitive advantage, you must have something to show for.

Sometimes it only takes one particular piece of information that you need that can make a huge difference in any given day or any given setting. Therefore, make reading a habit.

Motivational speaker and author Brian Tracy sums the importance of reading this way:
"If you read only one book per month, that will put you into the top 1% of income earners in our society. But if you read one book per week, 50 books per year, that will make you one of the best educated, smartest, most capable and highest paid people in your field. Regular reading will transform your life completely."

Knowledge properly applied becomes skills. According to research, money is with the top 10 percent in any given field. So, if you want to be financially successful aim to be at the top 10 percent in your field. Credentials (knowledge) and experience translated into skillset influence your earnings.[7]

There are certain skills you absolutely have to have to get to the top. Find the most valuable skillset in your industry and aim for mastery.

Everybody starts at the bottom and then they work themselves up. To go up, gain knowledge then apply the knowledge to turn into skill - knowledge and skill. Every time you develop a certain piece of knowledge and skills that people will pay you for, you move up ahead on your way to success.

When you stop learning, you stop moving and people will start to go past you. Everybody who wants to get to the top 10 percent just needs to keep on acquiring knowledge and skills pertinent to your field.

Clinical psychologist and Professor of Psychology, Jordan Peterson said that in terms of finding a job that fits you, to maximize your chances for success and well-being, find a stratum of occupation where you have an intelligence that would put you in the upper quartile. Then you will be the big fish in the small pond.

He added, "don't be the smartest one in the room either because that means you should be in another level but be in the middle where you have something to climb up to and once you've mastered it, go look for another job in your area of expertise where once again you are in the middle in terms of mastery.

As you go up the ladder of your job or career, the demand for fluidity of intellect becomes greater. Your ability to take in more information in a shorter amount of time becomes paramount and more importantly to apply the information in a way that adds measurable value to your company.

One way to exercise fluid thinking is to practice your ability to think fast on your feet at critical moments. First, practice in a safe environment with a mentor who can assist you in developing this skillset. Second, watch the people who are better than you, learn, apply and adjust to fit each circumstance. Third, get experience. Expose yourself to situations where you are forced to think fast and come up with strategies and solutions quickly. Fourth and the most important piece is to evaluate each experience and learn from your experiences.

There is little value to experience only. Experience without evaluation just means you are passing time. Evaluated experience, meaning you think about the whys, the wheres and the hows and whether your actions, behaviors, skillset, knowledge, etc. are sufficient or needs work, will contribute to your growth and add more to your storehouse of knowledge that you can pull from when faced with similar circumstances.

Force multiplier 2: Competence

"The only way to thrive in the future is to focus on what you love,
develop knowledge and skills in the service of your passion,
and be relentless in doing the work."
— Dragos Bratasanu, The Pursuit of Dreams:
Claim Your Power, Follow Your Heart, and Fulfill Your Destiny

Develop your competence. Competence is what you are gifted to do and what you do best. In developing competence, first you must know what your core strengths are. The how to is outlined below. Follow the steps and you will gain competitive advantage as you gain competence.

To develop competence:

- Know your core strengths

- Set goals to improve your skillsets

- Build your capacity

- Challenge yourself

- Attitude of giving 100% in whatever you do

- Expect excellence in yourself, strive to become better everyday

- Track your results

- Ask someone to mentor you

- Look for best practices and apply them

- Teach others

- Stay curious

Know your core strengths.

"Most people think they know what they are good at. They are usually wrong.... And yet, a person can perform only from strength"
– Business guru Peter Drucker

Your core strengths are the things that you do best and the positive traits you exhibit the most. To maximize these valuable resources, you must understand the resource within you. Ask your friends and the people closest to you. You may ask your boss or your co-workers. There are also multiple personality tests you can find online to help you determine your core strengths.

A good resource to start with is StrengthsFinder 2.0 by Tom Rath (https://www.gallupstrengthscenter.com/). Taking the assessment will give you an idea of the top 5 strengths you possess that when properly honed and directed will give you a competitive edge. Another resource is the fascination advantage, How the World Sees You, Discover Your Highest Value Through the Science of Fascination by Sally Hogshead.

One unconventional resource you may want to look into is Carol Tuttle's book, Dressing Your Truth, where you learn about your inner self and express yourself by the way you clothe yourself. I still use this resource on a regular basis to understand myself and others and it's fun!

Develop your core strengths. Look for ways to contribute to the company you work with using your core strengths. When finding a job, try to find a job that fits your core strength. You will find that the job is more rewarding compared to when you are working in an area you are weak in.

Set goals to improve your skillsets – SMART (Specific, Measurable, Realistic and Time-specific)

Set goals that would help you become more competent. When setting goals, they must be specific, measurable, realistic and time-specific. For example, to develop my competence in management and leadership I took specific actionable steps where I can measure the outcome of the decisions I made as a leader.

In instances where there is a problem in one area of the long-term care operations I am managing I would then need to plan, come up with a strategy, communicate and implement the changes and see if what was done was a success measurable by either increased revenue or decreased loss.

Build your capacity

Do more of what you are capable of doing now and add to your skillset whenever opportunities arise. Building your capacity takes time and it takes constant practice. Get input from others who know more than you know. Apply and practice, practice, practice! And then when opportunity arises, you are ready.

Increase your thinking capacity. Generate your own ideas or look for other people's ideas. Learn to critically assess ideas and once you've decided for the best one, apply it. Expand your thinking capacity by acquiring knowledge and evaluating the information you gathered.

Increase your emotional capacity. Evaluate emotions that does not serve you in reaching your goals. You have the ability to change your emotions by changing your perspective of things hence your experience.

Appreciate the difficulties you have gone through in your life, job, career or business. Make life's difficulties count by learning from them and let it serve as a guide to avoid future pitfalls.

Challenge yourself

Volunteer for assignments that you think are difficult but within your area of giftedness and passion. The more you do this, you will acquire more experience and greater intuitive capacity. You will experience exponential growth when you expose yourself to challenging assignments.

Attitude of giving 100% in whatever you do

The key word is attitude of giving. When you give of yourself, you also open yourself to possibilities. When you are fully immersed in whatever you are doing, you are captivating. There is bound to be someone who can make a huge difference in your life who will one day look at you giving your 100% and will say to themselves "look at this gem of a person I found!" This attitude will open doors of opportunities for you.

Expect excellence in yourself, strive to become better everyday

Expect excellence in yourself first then once you are able to do that and demonstrate excellence consistently, you can then encourage others to do the same. The top people in their field love their work and displays excellence.

Track your results

Collect data, analyze and strategize. It is only when you are analyzing the results that you can get better. As you become aware that certain actions or decisions led to unfavorable results, you will have a clearer understanding. Let this 'understanding' help you change your actions and subsequently, your results.

Ask someone to mentor you

I had mentors when I first started my career as a pharmacist. They were the people I called to ask for professional advice. They taught me how to think critically, how to respond to situations and how to make the right decisions. The times when I did not have a mentor were the times when my growth was slower than it should have been.

As my career progressed, I needed mentors who can guide me in leadership, entrepreneurial and business acumen – this is why I am part of the mentorship of the John Maxwell Team. I want to stack the odds on my favor. I invested in myself because I know that as long as I am growing, my future will remain bright and hopeful.

Look for best practices and apply them

Study organizations and individuals that do best, learn what it is that they do to help them stay on top of their game. Gather as many ideas, synthesize the ideas to see which ones are fit for your organization or whatever it is you are trying to do and apply the best idea.

Teach others

Teach others because not only you are contributing to the growth of others, your level of understanding increases when you teach. I find that it is when I have students that my mind is fully alert and involved in learning as well and because I am teaching I want to fully inform myself of the material and therefore my understanding increases.

Stay curious

Never let yourself believe that you know all there is to know about something or everything. Nobody knows everything perfectly. Staying curious will allow you to see things you would not normally see and understand things you would not normally understand if you believed yourself to have all the knowledge.

When you are curios, you are open to gaining knowledge. As you gain knowledge, your ability to make rapid decisions to give you the result you are looking for increases.

Force multiplier 3: Self-mastery

You are your own tool. Like a chef sharpening his most priced tool which is his knife you must sharpen yourself as well. When you focus on your strengths, you are in a better position to see and seize opportunities as they present themselves. As most people are content with being mediocre, you have more chances of success if you position yourself to be the best. Raise your skillset to a level higher than most people would go for. Sharpen your mind, seek things that stimulate your intellect and enable you to be faster and better.

Pick an area of your interest, develop your skillset, challenge your current capacities by placing yourself in a challenging environment to hone your skills until it becomes a part of you. This must be based not only in your area of interest but where you are naturally gifted. Natural giftedness plus training plus experience is a potent combination that would propel you to massive success.

Self-mastery is your ability to reframe the events and transform your inner experiences, so you can get to a state of resourcefulness. When you can do this quickly, it will help you become polished and confident. Confidence breeds success.

Oftentimes, I am called to employ the skillset of mastering my inner state. All of us who work directly with customers have a degree of self-mastery in this area, otherwise we would have been long gone from the company we worked for.

I can clearly recall when I represented my company in a joint project with one of the leading hospital and long-term care organization in Ontario. It was a very sensitive project and it required cooperation from high level executives of the organization we served. I was tasked with creating a set of protocol and procedures. It was the first time I ever participated in this kind of project and it was nerve-wracking. During meetings, I would present the draft, it would be picked apart word for word and questioned by none other than the Vice-President and Chief Medical Officer of the hospital and scrutinized by the committee. I would go back to the drawing board and "fix" it.

I would sit and agonize over this whole document for hours. This happened multiple times over the course of months. I was scared and embarrassed and thinking about what they could be possibly think about me. But when I really thought about it, I realized that the intention is to create a polished protocol and procedure that would work for the whole organization.

It was never about me, in fact they were helping me and the feedback was intended so that the project would be a success. When I changed my belief, I became more confident. I would still get nervous but never scared. I learned to master my state by changing my beliefs.

Develop an ability to master your state (state of confidence, state of feeling etc.) to get the results that you want. All state is a product of three things: what gets your attention or your focus, the meaning you attach to it or what you say to yourself and your physiology which is how you allow it to show up or feel in your body.[8]

When you are not in the most resourceful state, such as when you are feeling discouraged, down or depressed, anxious, angry etc. note where you place your focus. What is it that is bothering you and why? Ask yourself the question of 'what am I telling myself this means (self-talk)?', and 'how am I feeling and acting?'. Then switch perspective.

Stand outside of yourself and notice other things that are happening around you. Is it possible that there could be another meaning beside the one that originally bothered you? Look for objective facts. You may surprise yourself that what you originally thought about was a mistaken assumption after all.

When called to do a difficult task that makes you feel a little bit insecure, a little afraid, here is what you need to do. Adopt the right mindset. Tell yourself that this is a great learning experience for you. When you are learning it does not matter whether you pass or fail, what matters is what you've learned.

Project yourself into the future. Picture yourself doing the task with ease and confidence. This will help you get the confidence you need to go forward. Accomplishing a difficult task will give you confidence that you have the ability within you that will grow and expand under challenges. When you develop this attitude, you become unstoppable!

Transformation happens when you can change what you focus on at will and change what you say to yourself to put your body in its most resourceful state. When you learn this technique, you are free to change your actions and behaviors whenever needed. Imagine what you can accomplish with this in your tool belt.

Force multiplier 4: Influence

To be wildly successful you need to master the art of influencing people. It works in any single field that you choose. Be genuine and likeable. Get others engaged with whatever you are doing.

Some people are naturally gifted influencers. Influencing is an art that can be learned. We are constantly influencing and being influenced whether at home, at work, in school or at play. The basis for influence is communication and since communication is the basis for influence, here are ways to improve this aspect of your life.

When communication is seemingly flowing from one individual to another, this is what we call rapport. Successful people are masters at creating rapport. Rapport creates trust and confidence. When two or more people are in rapport they participate in conversations in such a way that responses are given freely.

There are certain techniques of creating rapport that can help increase your level of influence and I guarantee you that these techniques work if you practice them. These techniques have been tested and are found effective. They are used by the most successful people in the world.

Get ready to be blown away by this new insider's information!

People who are in rapport have a tendency to match each other's gestures, posture and eye contact much like two people involved in a dance. There are techniques to create rapport with anyone. You can do that by *matching* and *mirroring* the other person's body language and voice tonality. When done with sensitivity and respect, it can bridge the gap between you and the other person's model of the world creating an 'understanding'.

Picture yourself standing in front of a mirror, you move and the image in the mirror also moves the same way as you do facing the opposite direction. To mirror someone is to subtly imitate the way that person moves and behaves. Remember the key word is *subtle*. When *mirroring*, you may do the gesture that the other person is doing while the other person is speaking or do the same gesture when it is your turn to speak.

Matching is subtly imitating the person using the same side of the body they are moving. For example, if the person is tilting his/her head to the right, match it by tilting your head to the right side as well. Be careful not to make your movements noticeable or exaggerated as if you are mimicking the other individual as it can be considered offensive. You can also match body weight distribution and basic posture. A technique called cross-over mirroring is an alternative that is less noticeable where you match arm movements by small hand movements, body movements by your head movements.

Aside from physical gestures, matching is also done with words, voice (tone/voice pitch, timbre, tempo/cadence and volume) and breathing.[9]

There are differences in which people processes information. You can also match the way they process information and represents information to themselves. Some are detail-oriented while others are big picture thinkers. Others are more visual or process information by hearing or talking to themselves or moving. You would want to match whichever way they represent information to themselves for you to be a powerful communicator.

Practice makes perfect, so begin practicing with your friends and family and see the joys of wonderful communication!!!

Remember, *be subtle.*

Force multiplier 5: Personal Magnetism and Charisma

Be comfortable in your own skin. Pretending to be something else or someone else you are not makes you come across as inauthentic. People like genuine people. It is the key to connection and connection is the key to influence.

Make your innate personality work to your advantage. I used to think I have to hide who I truly am to get accepted by people around me but to shine, we must show our true selves. Only when we truly show up and are authentic that our personal power is projected to the world. People will respond in a positive way when you are genuine.

Some people are naturally friendly and can make anybody feel at ease and have a good time just by talking to them in their usual upbeat way. Be yourself at work at home or anyplace. I guarantee you that even with just your presence alone, you can make someone's day.

There are those who are naturally and more emotionally connected. They have a sensitivity to them that makes them attuned to their surroundings, other people's feelings and emotions. If you are one of these people, your gift of connectedness is needed in this world of fast-paced lifestyle and shallow social media relationships. For others who are more action and results-oriented, have a bigger than life vision and the ability to make it happen – the world needs you to create results that can change lives and inspire many.

If you are one who is drawn to the pursuit of perfection, inspire the rest of us to be better and become better and exceed the limits of what we think is our capacity.

You are uniquely you and you are uniquely equipped to contribute to the world around you. I hope you understand your value and I hope you use what you have to influence others to see the positives of life and to make an impact.

Now let us talk about you in the spotlight. Walk with a purpose. Powerful people always walk as if they have somewhere to go and something to do. To stand out from the crowd you must learn to exude personal magnetism and charisma. To exude personal magnetism and charisma you must be able to display presence, power and warmth.

Presence

Presence is simply your ability to be present and to be in the moment with the person you are speaking to. It signals engagement. Nobody wants to speak to someone who is not truly listening to them. Charismatic individuals, whenever they are with people, their focus is not on themselves but on the people. Be present when speaking to someone. Make appropriate eye contact. Body language is essential to establish presence. Men can exude presence and magnetism with shoulders squared, feet planted firmly on the floor. If you are a woman you can increase your presence by simply centering yourself, bringing your weight and focus in the womb space and practicing stillness.

In today's world, we have so many things going inside our head even when we are talking to someone. Practice stilling the clamor in your head and focus on the person in front of you. Be in the moment.

Voice and words

When speaking to an audience captivate them with your ability to move their emotions. Desire lies in the subconscious and emotions are products of the subconscious. When you move their emotions, you are closer to influencing them to do what you want them to do. Use your voice as a tool. Lower the timbre to exude authority and higher for playfulness. When conversing with people, convey words that shows warmth. When you show people that you truly care, it draws them to you.

Energy

Charismatic people carry a positive energy. They encourage, inspire and lift the people around them. Their energy is outward focused. Project confidence when you are in front of people especially when you are leading them or when you are representing your company. Use movement deliberately. To command a room, make your gestures bigger. If you are leading, take up space with your body language. Expand your energy by letting your awareness expand.

Dress for success

Represent yourself and the company you work for well. First impressions matter. People automatically evaluate you based on how you present yourself including your clothing. Have a couple of wardrobes reserved for situations when you need to bring your best self forward such as important meetings with clients or going to an interview.

Styles of Charisma

According to Olivia Fox Cabane, author of The Charisma Myth, there are 4 charisma styles. You can learn each of these charisma styles and choose to adopt them based on your personality, your goals and the situation you are in.

One is focus charisma which is primarily based on the perception that you are truly present in your encounter with someone. This kind of charisma makes people feel heard and understood.

Second is visionary charisma which inspires belief and confidence. Visionary charisma requires the ability to project complete conviction and confidence with a degree of display in passion on one's cause or vision.

The third one is kindness charisma which is based on warmth and confidence. It makes people feel connected, welcomed and accepted.

The fourth kind of charisma is authority charisma. Authority charisma is the most powerful form of charisma. It is based on the display of status and confidence where there is a perception of power and authority. People with authority charisma can make others believe that they have the power to affect our world.[10]

I encourage you to get to know yourself and find out what kind of charisma you possess, cultivate it and employ it to your advantage.

Force multiplier 6: Decision-making Ability

You may ask yourself what trait sets apart successful from unsuccessful people? It is the ability to make quick decisions and adjust their actions if the result is not the result they are looking for. It requires the ability to look at things objectively. But many people lack the ability to make quick decisions. Some even refused to make their own decisions preferring someone else to do the thinking for them. These kinds of people remain stuck in their lives and they wonder why where they are at. They blame others or outside forces for their circumstances. They blame their husbands or their wives, their kids, the government, the media etc., etc. They blame others instead of looking at themselves and changing what needs to be changed.

Decision-making is a skill. The more you practice the better you will be at it. The more correct decisions you make, your confidence in your ability to make the right ones increases. If you are afraid of making decisions, start smaller ones and as your confidence grows, make bigger decisions.

Ask those who have wisdom and expertise in the area you are making a decision in for their input. Ask multiple people you trust but be wise in whom you ask for input from. Only ask from people who have actually done it and have learned from their own mistakes. Listen to them then make up your mind to apply what is correct for your situation.

Force multiplier 7: Leadership Ability

Develop your leadership ability but first, lead yourself. Oftentimes people look at somebody who is successful and envy them. The thing with success is, you never really know the sacrifices and the risks that person took to get to where they are. We just see the result of all the years of training, hardships and difficulties. These people were able to lead themselves back up from failure after failure.

Once you can lead yourself, set the pace and lead. For example, when you want people to move fast, move faster...if you want a positive work environment, be the bearer of positivity. Create a pattern of success and results then others would be willing to follow you. Understand that leadership is both art and science.

Learn the technical aspects of leadership such as strategy, planning and finances. Practice the art of leading people through connecting, communicating, casting vision and motivation. Develop both and you will become a phenomenal leader.

Force multiplier 8: Love of Learning

Make a learning a priority. Learning should not end when you finish school. Strive to learn more skills. Develop your people skills, your planning and strategic ability, decision-making ability. Take courses. There are some online courses you can take for free or available for a small fee.

Ever since as a kid I was endlessly curios about the world and my curiosity has not diminished. I was always drawn to new advances in science and technology, the arts and psychology. I had a love of learning and so was a voracious reader. I would read anything I could get my hands on from magazines, books to volumes upon volumes of encyclopedia.

One time when I was nine years old, I ran out of things to read and I found a philosophical publication my parents had. It was in English. I could not understand what the words meant. I kept reading anyway in hopes of finding a word that was easy enough to understand that perhaps could shed light to whatever it was I was reading. Unfortunately, there was none but I was happy and satisfied because I encountered new words and thought that maybe in the future I will understand them.

Not knowing something just means you have an opportunity to learn something new! Sadly, in school we were not taught we can be smart if we choose to be. Our brains are built in such a way that as you learn more, you actually get smarter and smarter! As you learn your brain makes physical structures of proteins. Each new information gets wired into the existing network. Your brain makes protein connections much like highways to connect information. The more you use it, the faster the connection flows and your understanding and ability to make deductions increase.

Always try to learn new things. Read to keep up with advances in your field. Take up hobbies that are enjoyable and engaging. This way you can keep your neurons firing! Also, allow yourself to fail and learn from your failures.

When I fail, I ask myself why? What can I learn from this? How can I make the process better? How can I make myself better? How can I prevent this from happening in the future? As a manager, I teach my staff to ask themselves the same questions. I am growing, my staff is growing individually in capacity and skills, and our business is growing. We are being recognized as true partners in healthcare. Is learning from failure easy? Not in the least but when you do, you will benefit greatly.

When we keep our curiosity, we open ourselves up to sparks of creativity. We are all intelligent beings capable of forming and drawing new and never seen creative inventions and improvements for our lives and business. No one knows the future however, when you are growing your future remains optimistic.

Force multiplier 9: Networking

Personal contacts increase your probability of success. The number of people you know and the number of people who knows you in a positive way will influence how fast you move through the success lane.

Every opportunity in life is given by someone who gives you opportunity, opens the door for you, buys from you, hires your services or introduce you to someone who can do that for you. But you never know who that someone is, so the key is to keep expanding your network of people.

It is always the number of people you know and the number of people who knows you in a positive way that increases the probability of you meeting your success goal.

Networking is incredibly important if you want to experience massive financial success. Keep in this in mind and when you realize what you want out of your life, begin to associate with people who have what you desire. The reason being is that their way of thinking rubs off on you. As your thinking changes your actions change and therefore your results change.

Build credibility. In networking, you need to have credibility with people where they know you and trust you. Build relationship first before you ask for business. There are those people reaching out to others showing desperation, some would flat out even beg people to help them by buying their products or services. That is not the most effective way of doing business. It puts people off and I'm sure people avoid those kinds of interactions as it makes them uneasy.

Successful networkers tell others that when networking, it is important not to sell to them. Find out first what they like and try to help them. Ask 'Would it be of any value to you if I do this?'. Help them instead of selling to them.

Look for overlapping areas of interest and stay connected with each other. Dress the part so that the people will have the correct perception of what you want to convey to them about you and have a positive attitude. People love talking about themselves so always ask people about themselves to create connection when networking face to face.

Be generous with your network of people and you will never run out of job or business. This was true for me. As I helped others, they helped me. In fact, I had multiple job offers everywhere because I was genuinely connecting with people.

Never underestimate the power of generosity in networking. It is proven to be true that the more generous you are, the more opportunities you will be given. Many of the immigrants who became truly successful because of the strength and size of their network.

Dr. Ivan Messner founder of Business Network International gives a thorough training on principles of networking. His website is http://ivanmisner.com/.

Force multiplier 10: Your True Power Lies in Your Character

Character is simply defined by D.L. Moody as "Who you are when no one is looking." Character is who we are on the inside. Your character reflects your values. It reflects who you are and what you are made of. No one can take it from you.

Dr. John C. Maxwell said that talent may get you somewhere, but it is character that protects your talent. When you have consistency in your values, ideals, thoughts, words and actions, people can and will trust you.

I've been working in my industry for 13 years and had the opportunity to mentor and teach immigrant pharmacy students who wanted to be registered pharmacist in Canada. As I spent time with people who were like me, immigrants to a new country I was struck with the similarities we all had.

It didn't matter which country we came from. There were a few character traits that stood out to me that differentiated and gave us an edge. What we had in common were our perseverance, resilience and courage to face unfamiliar situations.

Finding a job, meeting new people from diverse cultures, learning new things and new ways of living are all challenging in and of itself. Add to that the absence of loved ones for support. Sometimes it can make you feel truly alone.

The fact that someone left their country of birth and away from their families to make life better for their loved ones say something much more to me about their character. They speak of love and dedication. It was not a surprise to me when my friends who came with me and went through the same journey became successful pharmacists and entrepreneurs.

If you are an immigrant reading this book, I truly do admire your guts and your courage to come to a new country to start a new life.

However, as much we have the character traits that allowed us to start anew, to be truly successful we must also grow in other areas of our character as well.

Initiative

"Success comes from taking the initiative and following up... persisting... eloquently expressing the depth of your love. What simple action could you take today to produce a new momentum toward success in your life?"
– Tony Robbins

Initiative is the ability to use your judgement to make decisions and do things without needing to be told what to do. Success requires that one must have initiative whether you work for someone or you are your own boss. The world has a way of rewarding those who act.

Imagine if you are all dreams and ideas with no action, it does not lead anywhere. You need to take initiative, take action!

As a leader, I am always on a lookout for people who shows initiative. I like having those kinds of people around because together we can accomplish something better than any one of us can do. Working with someone who has initiative enables us to aim higher and have bigger goals.

Companies reward employees who show initiative. For an entrepreneur, initiative will result in increased revenue and increased growth.

Courage

"When I dare to be powerful, to use my strength in the service of my vision, then it becomes less and less important whether I'm afraid"
- Andre Lorde

There is only one way to avoid criticism: Do nothing, say nothing and be nothing
- Aristotle

Rabbi Shmuley Boteach wrote in his book "Face Your Fear"

"Unless you conquer fear, it will conquer you. Fear not only prevent you from fulfilling your greatest destiny, but it threatens you of your very identity by destroying everything about you that is unique. To be afraid is to be transformed from a human being of destiny to creature of no future."

I read "Face Your Fear" book in 2006 and it had a profound impact on me. I was afraid of a lot of things but what I was most afraid of was thinking that at the end of my life, what would I look back on? Would I look back on my life filled with regrets because I did not dare to go after what I truly desire out of fear? I decided that I could not accept that fate.

From that time on I decided to try to do things I never tried before because of fear. I loved martial arts movies, so I learned taekwondo, wushu and kung-fu. I even joined one competition even though I was deathly afraid of getting beaten up and I did but it was worth it! Guess what? I even got two trophies out of that one competition, plus one broken toe and multiple bruises. It sure felt like I was hit by a log every time I got kicked but I was happy that I conquered my fear!

One windy day I got to " fly" a four-seater plane for a few minutes up. The small plane was vibrating and I was so stiff so the plane went up and up, the pilot told me to relax and the plane went down and down. The plane later landed sideways, that was scary!

I went for scuba diving and realized I was claustrophobic, hyperventilated and had to get out of the water. I swam in an open sea in Cancun to look at underwater sculptures all the while managing my fear of water because I cannot swim well. I went and did ziplining while feeling nervous and shaky, went the second time and felt exhilarated.

With three friends, I went on a trip to Kenya that forever changed me. We decided that we want to "make a difference". We went on a safari and visited a place where most people living there have AIDS, we held babies and children who were orphaned due to AIDS and who themselves have AIDS. I met wonderful people whom I admired for their courage, tenacity, perseverance, self-sacrifice and above all for their love. I was wrong in thinking I would make a difference, these people were the "real" difference maker, the children I met were the one who made a difference – they changed me.

And because I dared myself to step out of fear into courage that I am now writing this book and it took a lot of courage for me to write this book.

When we are afraid, we are the ones to ultimately suffer. You cannot be happy and fearful at the same time. Fear robs you of happiness. Living in fear is the surefire way of letting your dreams die unfulfilled.

Without courage, we will stay hidden on the safe zone. Those who are successful in this life look at fear in the eye and step by step went and did the things they were afraid to do at first.

Self-Confidence

Sometimes I find myself thinking that I couldn't be as good as the people born and raised in Canada because I did not grow up here, I didn't have the education that they have, and that somehow, I am lacking in my capacity. During those times, I let opportunities slip past me.

Thoughts backed by emotions become our reality. These thoughts of not enough are not true by the way. Those were only products of my imagination. I've seen my results and the results say the opposite, that I am more than capable. It took me a while to truly know and understand in my heart that you and me and "them" are all equal.

It is understandable that we are not comfortable doing something because it is new to us. But if we are not going to try we will never learn. It is okay not to be confident at first when you are just starting and learning but after some time you should be developing a measure of self-confidence. I am not saying that I got this, but I am still working on it. Let's work on this together shall we?

The question is how do we develop self-confidence?

First of all, you must develop skills. In my case, although I had a bachelor's degree in pharmacy in my own country, I still studied International Pharmacy Graduate Skills Program that was offered at the University of Toronto to learn and develop my skillsets to be comparable to that of Canadian pharmacy graduates. Then I went for studentship and internship to have experience with real-life settings. Once I got a job, I learned interpersonal skills and management skills. The funny thing was that as a student, the company did an assessment on me and concluded that I was not manager material. Little did they know that I had the "love of learning", the capacity to persevere and to be resilient.

So, learn the skills and when you have learned and mastered the skillsets required you will gain confidence.

Second, draw from your inner self the confidence that comes from a deep conviction that whatever life throws at you, you can and will handle it. Above all, know this and remember… you already have something to offer to the world that no one else can.

Third, gain successes. Start with small successes then go for bigger goals and succeed in them. This will cement your identity as someone who can make things happen. Write your successes in your journal to give you encouragement when you need it.

Fourth but not the least. If you believe in God, believe that you have a higher power backing you up. It will give you hope and courage to go forward even during the most difficult times.

Be confident and be bold. Let the world notice you.

Perseverance

"Permanence, perseverance and persistence in spite of all obstacles, discouragements, and impossibilities: It is this, that in all things distinguishes the strong soul from the weak."
– Thomas Carlyle

"It ain't about how hard you hit, it is about how hard you can get hit and keep moving forward. That's how winning is done."
-Rocky Balboa in the movie Rocky

All wildly successful people have gone through difficulties and hardships. The more successful they are, the more they have gone through the ups and downs, but they persevered during difficult times. They understood that between their dream and the realization of it requires sacrifices and a lot of sweat. People who are successful are not quitters. It is only the unsuccessful people who thinks that life should be always sweet and easy.

Many of the immigrants who come to a new country face hardships. Just remember that the more you persevere, the more you will get rewarded for your efforts. Keep the positive attitude and be willing to take risks.

Humility

"True humility is not thinking less of yourself;
it is thinking of yourself less."
— Rick Warren, The Purpose Driven Life:
What on Earth Am I Here for?

"It is unwise to be too sure of one's own wisdom. It is healthy to be reminded that the strongest might weaken and the wisest might err."
— Mahatma Gandhi

What is humility? Humility is knowing who we truly are and accepting our strengths with gratitude and our limitations without judgement. It is looking at the world around us with appreciation that we are part of it and interconnected with each other. Humility is being honest with ourselves and others knowing that we are imperfect yet not devaluing ourselves with the knowledge of our imperfections. Humility stems from self-confidence - a deep knowing of oneself.

We can show humility in the workplace by admitting our mistakes, seeking advice and input, willingness to collaborate and share the stage with others so to speak, willingness to hear other people's point of view, willingness to speak last and not hug the limelight. Humility also shows in your generosity in praising others do well.

Respect for Self and Others

"Respect for ourselves guides our morals, respect for others guides our manners."
- Laurence Sterne

I had an immigrant student once. I did not know him but agreed to take him in since he had the courage to approach me and asked me to be his preceptor and train him for four months as a prerequisite to him taking the pharmacy equivalency exam. He was a successful pharmacist in his own country. Later I learned that he had a major problem. He looked at my staff as if they were below him. He kept on acting as if he was better than them and would command my staff to work as if he was the boss. It created a major problem with the rest of my staff. This student became a pharmacist and got a job that eventually fired him in a matter of months. I suspected he got fired for his attitude.

You cannot command respect, you earn respect. You earn it by being respectful to others, it does not matter what position they have within your company. You earn respect by valuing others.

Integrity

"Goodness is about character - integrity, honesty, kindness, generosity, moral courage, and the like. More than anything else, it is about how we treat other people."
- Dennis Prager

*"With integrity, you have nothing to fear, since you have nothing to hide.
With integrity, you will do the right thing, so you will have no guilt."*
- Zig Ziglar

Integrity simply means you do what you said you would do. People who have integrity can be trusted. People who do not have integrity cannot be trusted and if people cannot trust you then your chances of success are limited than it could have been.

Avoid gossiping about others behind their backs. Talking bad about others not only destroy people's reputation but yours as well. When you talk, talk words of encouragement and words that would lift the person you are talking to. Talk as if every word you say matters and if it is supposed to matter, then it needs to be something that would build others up. Be someone who makes the world a better place.

Diplomacy and Tact

*"Be a craftsman in speech that thou mayest be strong,
for the strength of one is the tongue, and speech is
mightier than all fighting."*
— Ptah-Hotep

"Tact is the knack of making a point without making an enemy."
— Isaac Newton

Diplomacy is the art of effectively dealing with people with thoughtfulness, discretion and sensitivity. Diplomacy and tact require the ability to assess the situation and create win-win situations. Not everyone is born with a fine-tuned ability for diplomacy and tact.

However, this skill can be learned. Some people are naturally good at it but some not quite. They require empathy, understanding and ability to respond appropriately to further relationships. Someone must be able to see the other party's views and feelings to be effective in this area.

To improve your skillset in this particular area, develop cultural intelligence. Cultural intelligence (CQ) is the ability to recognize shared beliefs, values, attitudes, and behavior of a group of people and, most importantly, to apply this knowledge toward a specific goal is critical.

Your ability to understand differences in how others think, behave and makes decisions, view the world and interpret actions will help you in creating strategies and options on how best to engage them to achieve your own objectives. (Spencer, 2009)[11]

Take Care of Yourself – Work Hard, Play Hard

You are the most valuable commodity in your world. You are the most valuable investment. If you have a possession like a car or for women a purse that you like so much, wouldn't you take good care of it? Yet, some of us take our bodies, our physical, emotional and mental health for granted. We think that our bodies will always serve us and that we will always be one hundred percent on top of the game. But that is not the case. When we are tired and overworked, we are not as resourceful or positive. When we are not physically well, we cannot function to the best of our ability.

In all your pursuits, do not forget to take care of yourself. Love yourself. Spend time and money on yourself. Take care of your emotional health, mental health and physical health. Take time to rest and reset your mind and body, read for pleasure, go to a spa or massage, take nature walks or go camping. Sing! Dance! Pick up a hobby! Do what give you joy. Reserve money for fun times with friends and family or take a vacation.

It is good to unplug from all the hustle and bustle of life once in a while and refresh your being. This way, when you come back you are energized and ready to go again.

The Happiness Factor

Write on this page, what makes you happy....

Now, do what makes you happy....

Beware of Quick Rich Schemes – There Is No Substitute for Hard Work and Dedication

Let me tell you a story of this one guy who comes to our store to buy lottery tickets almost every single day. In a day, he could spend up to a hundred dollars on lottery tickets and on one especially lucky day he won twelve thousand dollars! What a lucky guy indeed! We were happy for him most especially since he was wheelchair bound and has physical disability. There are those who won millions in lottery but only a few people in the world are lucky in this way.

Most people who have wealth have gotten it through trial and error, have accumulated knowledge, applied their knowledge to create wealth, put a lot of effort and planning into creating and gaining wealth. They are willing to do what is difficult and sometimes seemingly impossible to turn the odds of winning their way.

Independently wealthy people (those who have gone from having nothing to acquiring and sustaining wealth) developed certain habits and skills that allowed them to gain even more wealth and it takes time.

It takes time, patience and skills. I've been to many seminars where they teach you to get rich quickly and you know what? They never worked! I paid thousands of dollars for these courses and they left me with thousands of dollars of debt.

The reason why they did not work was because I did not know myself enough. Those methods were unsustainable and did not fit my lifestyle or my highest values.

The things that matter to us are never the ones that show quick results. Be patient and persevere. There is no substitute for hard work. Take note however that in this day and age, hard work, grit and sheer willpower by themselves no longer works.

We are in the age of acceleration of information and technology where information and technology rapidly change. Therefore, we need to have a change in mindset in the way we view ourselves in relation to the world around us.

If what was previously sought after was people's ability to memorize information and apply it, since we have information readily accessible what is now highly valued is one's ability to problem solve, respond to needs of the customers, ability to create new systems and processes, develop strategies to solve myriads of issues in your chosen field of occupation.

If you want to be a wealthy entrepreneur, study the most successful entrepreneur and do what they do. If you want to be the most successful sales person, study all the sales and marketing books you can lay your hands on and hit the pavement! Wealthy people build their empires brick by brick, concept by concept, skill by skill.

When you develop yourself and engage your creative side, your logic and reasoning, there is no telling what heights you can achieve.

Now it is time to build your future. The sky's the limit.

PART 5
INTERVIEWS

The following are transcripts of interviews of successful immigrants. They shared about their lives in Canada and what it is like to be an immigrant, the challenges they faced and how they went about overcoming those challenges. There are many more whom I have interacted and observed who are not featured in these pages. It is my hope that as you read the interviews, you learn from them as you learned from me.

Kundan Joshi
Founder & CEO, TheAppLabb | 2018 Top 25 Canadian Immigrants | 2018 RBC Entrepreneur of the Year | Top 150 Extraordinary Canadians | 2016 Innovator of the Year - Transformation Awards| 2017 ICCC Technology Achiever

Kathryn: Hi Kundan, thanks for agreeing to this interview. Would you mind telling me about yourself?

Kundan: I'm 37, I've been in this country for about 18 years now. It was year 2000 when I came to Canada. Earlier part of my life until 20 years I was in India. That is where I was born and brought up and my family decided to move here. I continued my engineering course in Canada. I went to University. During university I started my business.

After I graduated I started a moonlighting, I have a full-time job during the day and in the evening continued my business and eventually move on to start the business full time. I've been fortunate to grow it step-by-step through the process where now today the AppLabb company has grown to have 70 employees across 8 different global offices. More importantly we continued to work on products which are innovative and continue to contribute towards how we can use innovation and technology towards improving human experiences and making people life easier, making people life simpler, helping our client's company prosper by differentiating themselves through technology and innovation.

Kathryn: When you were in India, were you already an engineer and you studied engineering again here or how was it for you?

Kundan: I had to repeat 1 year. I studied engineering in India but I wasn't able to get credits for that. I started my engineering from scratch so I lost 1 year there. But I retrospect if I get the credits, the programming language there is different than here. In essence, it was worth it.

Kathryn: What made you go into entrepreneurship? Are you a family of entrepreneurs or you have it in you to be an entrepreneur?

Kundan: I didn't think I would be an entrepreneur to be honest. I didn't grow up thinking I would be. One side, my mom's side of family have been entrepreneurs, my dad's side of family I don't think anyone have been an entrepreneur ever so I didn't really grow up thinking I would be an entrepreneur. It all changed during one summer job to be very honest.

After my first year of engineering here in Canada, part of my summer job was a sales job and as started that first job I just realized that I was good at sales and I did very well. Then I went back to university. I was making maybe $100,000 in 3 months just by selling a lot so my boss then didn't want me to leave. He was like 'You are my best guy, I don't want you to leave. Even after graduation you won me hundred thousand in a year'. So I proposed and I said, 'I want to continue my studies but I can start a branch for you in London, Ontario where I studied'. So that was my first entrepreneur gig which came out of the fact that my sales job made me feel confident that I could go out and could start something that I could help people.

I started out the business while I was studying and that gave me a flavor of entrepreneurship and after that I just couldn't think of not being an entrepreneur. I couldn't think of just doing a job for the rest of my life.

Kathryn: That is really cool. So it was kind of like you just tried something and by accident you've realized that you were good in something.

Kundan: Yeah, exactly. I mean I always enjoyed helping people and finding solutions to people's problems. I didn't call that entrepreneurship at that point I just called it, 'I enjoy helping people'.

Actually, in university I did that. in college I did that, throughout high school in India I did that, so I always did that. But with entrepreneurship I just realized that it's something that I cannot just think of but I can actually implement and help people through that process in essence which is why the fourth business we tried was in services as well because we truly enjoyed seeing the benefits of working towards a particular plan. So the service was always ingrained in terms of what we do, in terms of helping people out.

I didn't think of it as entrepreneurship but that just made me realize again that yeah, I always have it in me. I always enjoyed talking to people, I always enjoyed finding solutions to people's problems and now I can do that by actually creating a product, creating something which is also ingrained in becoming an engineer. An engineer is about creating, creating something new. It just was a mesh-up of different worlds that I was part of, enjoyment of helping, technology and engineering and sales. They all contributed towards sort of me realizing that tech entrepreneurship is what I would like to do for the rest of my life.

Kathryn: That's cool because when you think of engineers they don't necessarily have the skillset of sales, but you are sort of a hybrid of the creative engineer and sales so that makes it really different. When you started the business, what were the challenges you've encountered?

Kundan: One of the biggest challenges is capital obviously. When I came to the country, I had student debt, I had to take care of my family as well, family as in my parents who were new immigrants as well who did not go to university in Canada so they had a lot more challenges than myself and finding the proper jobs here. I have to make sure I'm taking care of them, I'm taking care of my student debt and trying to accomplish this dream of mine.

Initially for a few years I had to do a full-time job for the same reason I couldn't get into business. I don't have the capital to do that so the first five years of my business I was doing a full-time job 9 to 5 and running my business 5 to 4am. That was my schedule for almost five years. That was very challenging. I can't really meet too many clients after 5pm necessarily. You have to make sure you're still balancing it out. That sort of made me realize that I need to start up a team in India because my eight hours of night to work I could hire someone here. Again, I need to find solutions towards the challenges I was facing.

My first recruits were in India. I had an old apartment building which my family owned so I rented it out to a developer who lived there and worked for me as well. It worked out that way. It was very challenging and a lot of long hours, a lot of hard work. I had no capital. Pretty much any revenue or sales had to go back to investing in my own business. A lot of challenges initially. As a new immigrant it's hard to get loans from bank as well especially when you have a student debt and so on. It was challenging but obviously I wouldn't have gone through the hardships if I didn't enjoy it. I enjoyed entrepreneurship. I enjoyed having the ability to help people, to find solutions, to create new products, to use innovation, and to use my sales side towards benefiting a bigger purpose.

Kathryn: Have you encountered any difficulties other than financial? For example, some immigrants experience discrimination or some prejudice.

Kundan: Hmmm, most challenges exist everywhere regardless whether its race or whatever. I've never really identified that as a challenge or never acknowledge it as a challenge because it's people at the end of the day, right? Whether it's a client or a person, at the end of the day it's your responsibility to make that connection to make sure that you are able to create a bond of trust. Because of backgrounds, if that is a gap in creating that trust, it's a challenge. But it's a challenge that can be overcome that needs to be overcome obviously right? Maybe that challenge didn't exist if I was doing this business in India but the fact is I'm doing it here and Canada is a much better place to do business. It was just a matter of identifying that challenge and crossing it.

If you acknowledge that as a problem, then you'll always look at it that way. I can't say that with assurance that oh this was okay, prejudice or so on, it's very challenging. At the end of the day it is two people. Even with the same race, same background, brothers can have challenges working with each other. When you have different backgrounds, different interests, different ways of interpreting things, obviously those challenges exist and it's up to us to make sure we understand the motivations of the other people, how are we helping them in accomplishing their goals and making sure whether it's with your employees, with your partners, with your clients, it's always a win-win right? When we start thinking about our win, we start thinking about the other person not helping me, which is not the case. We have to make sure that the other person is winning. Even if some people, you might help them win and they're not able to give it back. But in other cases when you help them win and they help you back that those twenty percent of the people that will give it back is good enough for you to be successful in life.

Kathryn: I like what you said that it's up to you if you acknowledge prejudice or not because some people they get stuck in that thinking so they are not able to get out of their situation or not able to move and I like what you said that it's always about the other person. How can you help them? How can you help them overcome so you are not really focused about yourself but you are focused about service so that helped you get through this and you don't even think about this as a challenge, you just think about it as two people having a conversation, having a transaction. I like your attitude that you don't really think about it as a challenge, but you think about it as okay, let's create communication which is the important part.

Kundan: I mean, every challenge and opportunity is an opportunity to learn something new. It's an opportunity to create something new that sometimes it works and sometimes it doesn't work. But even if it doesn't work you'll actually learn a lot more from it than when it works. The worse thing is when it starts working but then not really because in that case you don't even learn much nor do you progress much. You would rather fail and fail hard and fail early so that at least those challenge help you learn a lot faster, right?

Kathryn: That's cool. Yeah, that is actually one of the things that I talked about in my book that if you are not going to fail then you are not going to learn so might as well do it now, do it fast and then you learn something. Other than that, what helped you overcome the challenges that you experienced?

Kundan: I think attitude is the most important thing. I mean yeah, there are challenges when you move to a new country, there are challenges when you are starting a business. We should feel blessed and thankful to be in a country which is accepting and really has a great atmosphere to live, to work, to do business right? So, we need to look at those, identify and acknowledge those as blessing in essence, or as advantages and use that as a fuel towards mitigating any challenges that come into play.

I think that is the most important aspect that yeah sure there are challenges but what happens is when we are overcoming challenges and that is what we identify and acknowledge as challenges we're only looking basically at the areas which needs work or improvement so in a way we are going to that negative mindset where we are looking at the negative side of the picture. We stop identifying things that have worked and only look at things that needs to be worked on, right? It's more of an attitude check where any challenge that comes your way whether it's a financial challenge, whether it's a people challenge, whether it's any other, you identify that as a loving opportunity, you count your blessings on the things that are working for you and that is a regular challenge right?

Every time, every day I see new challenge or a new problem I guess, your mind's instinct is to identify that as a problem and say 'oh shoot now what do we do?' You almost need to train your mind that if something like that happens, you start thinking about, 'wait a minute your mind is right away identifying those challenges but we completely ignored the ten things that went right that day, the ten things that went right to last day'. You're only looking at the two things that went wrong yesterday and today. It's not necessarily right to ignore them. Identify them as things to be worked on, as challenges to be taken on, and opportunities of learning to be worked on while making sure that you also acknowledged what is going right. It's a validation that you're going on the right path, there are couple of obstacles, now let's find a solution towards how can we do that. Do I need to learn more? Do I need to find someone as a partner who can help me find those challenges? Is there solution in getting together, thinking with clear mind, unbiased mind and trying to figure out a solution in essence, right? So that's pretty much what I go through with any challenges that I faced.

Kathryn: Have you always been a positive thinker or that's something that you learned?

Kundan: I think I've always been a positive thinker but there have been cases where failures make you not think as positively anymore so I can't say I've always stayed a positive thinker. As a child, I think I was a positive thinker. When I started the business, I was very positive. During the entrepreneurial journey, there were a lot of loads, there were a lot of challenges, and some of them make you question your purpose, make you question your direction, make you question what's going on and I realized during those times for the first time I was letting my negative thoughts overpower my positivity. That was the realization that made me change my thinking again and make sure to take the right perspective. Staying positive is going to pull you through everything. It's the positivity that's going to make sure you climb the heights. Erasing the negativity is important but when you focus on erasing negativity you're dwelling your mind in negativity. Whether you're erasing it you're still letting into negativity so think positive and everything will lift you up.

Kathryn: In low times how do you encourage yourself? Is there something specific that you do?

Kundan: A couple of things I would say. One is just to clear your mind, right? That's very important. For every person it is different. Some people are working out, some people do it by meditating, some people do it by various other means. Usually it is doing something that you enjoy doing. Whatever that meditative state is for you. For me it's multiple different things. I'll meditate, I'll spend time with my family, I'll have some good laugh. Those kinds of things can help clear your mind because you want to declutter your mind, right? The second thing is acknowledgement. Well actually before even acknowledgement the second thing is reinforcing where are you going, what is your reason, what is your purpose in life, what is that why, why are you doing all of this, because the challenges seem very heavy when the purpose is left without direction. But when you know that this is where you're going and you are sort of where you are on that journey and the challenges you're facing it's an easy justification for all those challenges. When you say 'oh wow, I did not sleep for three days straight while trying to study for the exam', it is very difficult to motivate yourself to do that. But when you know the exam so well or you accomplished your goal in life and so on, it becomes a lot easy. Your mind justifies that really well.

Your mind is able to sort of keep that positive mindset to do that. So, the second thing is just validating that, okay where are we going, reminding yourself what is that goal. How clear is the vision is very important especially on those times because if there's no clarity, when your vision is getting cluttered, then those vision will be 'okay I know I'm doing it to be successful, I'm doing it to make a lot of money, that's okay'. But when it becomes hard that ambiguous vision of being successful is not good enough or having money is not good enough. Money is not good enough of a factor to say okay do I really need to do all these hardwork again for fifteen more days, fifteen more months or years or whatever that is. It becomes really difficult to justify that. Reinforcing that, reminding yourself of that is very important and then putting things in perspective based on that that you know what? What are these challenges, what are the perspective of these challenges, as far as my journey is concerned. What are the positives that happened in perspective of what my journey is concerned and as a result where am I, where am I in terms of where I was and where am I today in terms of not just my positioning but also my mindset where I was and how much have I learned through all these challenges and how aligned I am from my mind state perspective towards my goals. The physical mindset and the mental and spiritual mindset, both of them, how well are they aligned towards what I'm going to do so it helps you make sense of things and put things in perspective.

Kathryn: I like what you said about having clarity of your purpose and that money is not enough of a factor for people to do something but if you are focused on your purpose then you are more inclined to actually do it even though it's hard. Clarity of purpose is very important otherwise, we can go into negative state and go into a spiral because we don't know what our purpose are and we are not clear on what we need to do so thank you for those points. What advice would you like to give to the immigrants who are coming here, or have been already here and are struggling, what would you like to say to them?

Kundan: Ah, so one is again the mindset. Don't be overpowered by the challenges that you face. I mean, humans don't necessarily like change. We are conditioned to get into our comfort zone very easily right? As a new immigrant entrepreneur and if people want to pursue entrepreneurship there are two forms of getting stuck in our comfort zone. One, you are in a totally new place, which you don't understand probably the customs, the culture, the language, all those challenges are there as barriers and then on top of that for the entrepreneurs there are millions of unknowns of becoming an entrepreneur. I mean if you are afraid of stepping out of your comfort zone I mean you can be an immigrant and afford to do that. You've already put that, you've already taken that giant leap of coming to a new country. Not many people can do that because they are very attached to where they are from. It's very difficult for them to shift their mind. The fact that you've taken that step, you're already halfway there. Now don't stop at that. If you stop right now saying now okay I've done it, I can't adjust anymore so all of a sudden you're giving your mindset a shock. Because you've already moved completely away now you have to make sure you continue to stay away from your comfort zone.

You have to expose yourself to the new culture, meaning that I'm an Indian with an Indian background coming to Canada and hence I stick with my Indian group of friends. That's not really coming out of your comfort zone; making sure that you're really engaged into the culture, engaging into activities that every Canadian does.

It could be of any culture in essence, making sure you are exposing yourself, enjoying that experience, enjoying is important, embracing the new country. There's no harm in engaging and experiencing what people are doing in this country, making sure you're exposing yourself to that. I mean you might feel out of place, you might feel that I don't know what to say but you have nothing to lose.

You need to train your mind to expose yourself out of the comfort zone and that mindset shift is the start of other things that you need to do. If you are of a particular profession and you come here now you know that there might be a challenge where that profession is not acknowledged because you need to study more or your education back home or your experience back home was not enough.

So those are challenges but by implementing the first thing, by exposing yourself out of the comfort zone, that's when you're actually be able to engage with people who are working in that field. Whether that means you're getting mentorship from some of them, whether that means volunteering in some of the organizations of your industry, or if that means volunteering in some companies that are in the same path as yours. Whatever that could be, exposing yourself in whichever way possible, along with continuing with your job and so on. That'll make sure that you are ingrained in what being in that industry means in this new country.

Some immigrants might have a challenge from the language, some from the job perspective, some from the entrepreneur, or whichever that is, but that I should say the essential aspect. Make sure you expose yourself, make sure you integrate, truly integrate into the culture into the society and make sure you stay out of your comfort zone as far as the career is concerned so that when you start your vision that okay, I moved to this country, I want to be the best lawyer in Canada or I want to be in a job of what my true profession is and excel at it. You expect that vision to yourself now work backwards.

Sure, there could be challenges where okay I cannot get the job today hence I have to work somewhere. I have to let's say work at Tim Horton's right now or work in whatever job right now but don't let go of that. Don't get comfortable doing that job at Tim Hortons or working as a cab driver. Don't get comfortable doing that because you have to. Because your vision is still important.

You can still accomplish your vision as I have mentioned for myself. I wanted to pursue my business when I got out from the university actually I wanted to have a double major in business out of university. I wasn't able to start my business right after that but I found a way by working full time which I had to. I don't have a choice but still pursuing my dream in the evening by making sure I don't lose that hunger in myself to become an entrepreneur, I don't lose that vision. If I stopped doing that or have forgotten that, I would have settled for life which in the long run I would not enjoy or I would not be proud of. But by continuing on the path whether as on the side, whether as volunteer, whether it's in the evening, whether it's on weekends, whatever that means but staying on that path, you will eventually accomplish your goal and depending on how passionate you are of your vision about your purpose the faster you will achieve it and the further along you will go.

Kathryn: Have you always been a big thinker or is that something your learned or you picked up?

Kundan: I'm a big thinker, but I can't say I have clarity in thoughts. Probably as a child I said yeah I want to be the next Bill Gates, so from that I'm a big thinker but I did not know the path to get there. I didn't even know I wanted to be an entrepreneur, I thought by doing something and coding my way through I'll become the next Bill Gates. So, clarity of thought is important as well. That okay what does that exactly mean, where exactly do you need to go. I don't think that came naturally to me. I have to train my mind to really make sure that I'm able to visualize my vision, visualize my goals, where exactly I'm headed because mind processes that in a certain way.

When you are in a tough spot or have a tough month and you want to make yourself wake up in the morning those visual pieces will motivate you and help you spring out of bed. Yeah, I know it was a tough month, it was a really tough day yesterday and I have to face challenges today as well but do I have it in me to motivate myself that my body by itself wakes up in the morning and pushing hard right from the first breath that yes, I want to do this. I'm going to do this. So that clarity of thought helps your mind to really do that. But there some days when I wake up and say to myself 'oh man I'm going back to sleep'. I have to train my mind, 'what am I doing here?', I'm thinking, I'm not visualizing. I'm not visualizing where my journey is, I am not thinking where my directions is, what my purpose is. When I'm able to start visualizing that, I'll probably slack of for a few minutes then I get back to my feet and make sure I push myself.

Kathryn: I heard that this the technique that most successful people do and it looks like you've mastered it.

Kundan: Well, I have not mastered it yet. There are so many days that I go back and hit the snooze button (laughs).

Kathryn: (laughs) But you actually do visualize and that is a very good tip for the rest of us who doesn't do that because it starts from the inside and not somebody telling you what to do so you are your own motivator basically. Thank you very much for this interview. Even though this is only thirty minutes or so, there is so much that you've talked about that are very helpful and I think I will again listen to it and really digest what you've said. Again, thank you for your willingness to help the other immigrants like me and others, thank you so much.

Major Cecilia Reyes, Registered Pharmacist
Canadian Armed Forces
2014 CPhA International Leadership Award

Kathryn: Major Reyes, thank you for taking the time to be with me and agreeing to this interview tonight. I wonder, how long have you been in Canada?

Maj. Reyes: I came to Canada 2001 in August

Kathryn: What made you decide to come to Canada?

Maj. Reyes: Well, there's not a lot for us as pharmacists back home right, and the economic and political situation back home wasn't very good so I said, 'nothing is gonna happen with me here that's going to advance me in anything', that's why I decided to move out. I first went to Singapore but before I accepted the job in Singapore I already knew I was going to Canada because my application has already been sort of accepted by the Canadian embassy or the visa office so that time before I went to Singapore to work I already have a notice that I will just be waiting for a couple of months to get the visa or for the visa to be released to come here to Canada. I went to Singapore and I didn't finish the contract because I have to come to Canada already. Basically, I went to Singapore on the October of 2000 and then left in Singapore on July 2001 and I came to Canada August 2001 as a landed immigrant.

Kathryn: Can you tell me, in terms of someone who worked in two different countries, what was the difference between you being in Singapore and you being here in Canada?

Maj. Reyes: Well, there was not a lot of difference. Singapore is very westernized and even the way they do business in pharmacy. The way pharmacists practice in Singapore is pretty similar to Canada. Singapore follows the British way of practicing pharmacy so there's not a lot of difference. That's where I basically learned those counseling techniques and patient care that was my first exposure to that because you know we don't have that sort of pharmacy practice back home. We were hired as technicians but we did pharmacist jobs except for providing patient education to cancer patients and mental health patients and that's it. Everything else we do as what pharmacist there would. We did a couple of weeks training with their drug information pharmacist on counseling techniques, patient care techniques and we even had exams pretty much every week. Kind of like what we were doing in the Canadian Pharmacist Skills (CPS) program. I did that in Singapore before I left. I spent about 9 months in Singapore before I left for Canada.

Kathryn: Did that help you then to become a licensed pharmacist in Canada because you have that background?

Maj. Reyes: In a way yes, because it wasn't really that new for me anymore meaning the time when we did CPS and when we did the exams. I mean, even though we were allowed to do counseling, it was not the full capacity. Solving cases and things like that, applying therapeutic knowledge wasn't really the same. It's definitely different here in Canada.

Kathryn: So you came to Canada, you became a pharmacist but how did you get to the army?

Maj. Reyes: When I came to Canada I had to do the same thing as everybody else. When I landed I didn't have any pharmacy-related jobs right away. I worked in a café for a couple of months. Actually, I decided already that I'm going to take the exams. There's no future in what I was doing. I was basically wasting my time so I have to take the exam right away. The first opportunity that basically I could take the exam I took it. I came here August 2001, I took the evaluating exam January 2002 and then I went from there. I took the CPS and I get licensed in 2003. From 2003 I was with Rexall or PharmaPlus at that time. I started with them as a pharmacy assistant and I worked my way up until being the manager and then I decided that I am not very comfortable with Toronto. Toronto that time was too much for me. I kind of needed some change so you know our friends are in the North or Simcoe area like Barrie and Orillia so maybe I could look for a house in Barrie and so I did. I stayed in Barrie from 2006 up until my posting to Ottawa. In 2006 I was still with Rexall and then in 2007 I decided to go to the recruiting center in Barrie actually. I've been wanting to join in the military since I was in the university back home but "nanay" (mother) won't allow me. During that time female participation in Philippine Military Academy (PMA) was very new at that time. It was just the second year that basically they allowed female participation in PMA so "nanay" didn't want me to join because you know, there's a lot of involvement, there's a lot of hazing and some other thing. But I took the exam - the entrance exam but I didn't pursue it because she wouldn't allow me. So when I had my license in Canada to practice pharmacy I've been wanting to join already. I called the recruitment center and they said there are three mandatory requirements to join the military. One, you have to be a citizen of Canada. Number two is you have to be medically fit. Number three for pharmacist is you have to have a license to practice or you need to be accepted to a pharmacist school or they're not gonna accept you as a pharmacist or as a pharmacy student. Anyways, during that time I didn't have my citizenship yet. Actually, after getting my citizenship my friend Ricardo and I (he went with me to the oath-taking ceremony) the first thing we did after is we went to the recruiting center in Sheppard and Yonge. We just wanted to see how things are or see what's out there, so we went, and I think we had the shock of our lives. I didn't think I could do it, it's too much, it's too hard, it's too complicated, it's too difficult so I said, nah, probably not. I was in Toronto still that time, that's around 2005 I think or early 2006. I moved to Barrie late 2006 then I actually got bored of my life in community retail pharmacy, so I finally decided I'm just gonna go to the recruiting center and see what they have for me. First thing that they did when I said I'm a licensed pharmacist practicing here in Canada, what sort of job can I apply for here? Right away they contacted the recruiting manager for pharmacists because in the Canadian Armed Forces that time there was an especially high demand for pharmacists, so they took me in right away. I had sort of a luncheon meeting with the recruiter, that was around June and a couple of exchanges of emails and all that stuff and then I was loaded to the basic military officer qualification. I got sworn in I believe it was in June as well then I started training mid or late of August. I was in **Saint-Gabriel-de-Valcartier**, Quebec for sixteen weeks up until the second week or third week of December.

Kathryn: So that was physical training?

Maj. Reyes: It was a bootcamp. I trained with people in different trades. I have a pilot in my class, infantry officers, intelligence officers, nurses, public affairs officers, naval officers, artillery officers, engineers and combat engineers as well. Well, we're pretty much a good bunch, a good mixture of different trades. I basically trained with them for the basic training and then after that I went back to Barrie. My first posting was in Borden, Ontario 20-30 minutes away from Barrie. That was my first posting as a pharmacy team lead for the clinic. It was from 2008 to 2011. From 2011, I was posted to Ottawa in the headquarters under drug affairs. Pharmacy policy and standards, that was my job back then. I don't know I had so many jobs but the main function was doing drug use evaluation.
Kathryn: And this is for the military?

Maj. Reyes: Well, the military paid for my education as well. The military paid for me to go to University of London to do the pharmacy vigilance course so I need to be posted to a position where I could utilize that skill. Anyway, so I became staff officer number 3, drug use evaluation, and I took over recruiting as well. Actually, before I went to Pharmacy Policy and Standards I was with medical operations and plans. That was my first year in Ottawa with J4. Joint number four (4), it means logistics. J4 is for medical logistics. My position then was medical operations and plans number 2. Main function is basically to ensure that operations worldwide would get the medications and medical supplies that they need so it's more like coordination with the deployed Ops and their medical supply needs and also the other job is the procurement of medical countermeasures.

Kathryn: Is it safe to say that you had the dream even though before you came to Canada?

Maj. Reyes: I just wanted to join the military back even when I was back home in Philippines so I joined and then after that I went to pharmacy policy and standards. I was there for only maybe two months and then I was called to do training from October to December and then I got deployed to Afghanistan in January 2013. I stayed in Afghanistan for six and a half months.

Kathryn: You did a lot of things….

Maj. Reyes: Yup, a lot of things. A lot of things that you can never imagine I did them all. When I came back from Afghanistan I went back to pharmacy policy and standards, same position and all. I came back 2013 and I stayed there up until 2015 February then my boss told me that I'm gonna be posted to Petewawa at CMED. That's the Central Medical Equipment Depot. Of course pharmacy ops are taking care of couple of things, medical kits, biomedical technologies, customer care service. So CMED is basically a unit that supports the operations directly so that's somewhat like the logistics warehouse.

Kathryn: What were you doing in Afghanistan? Was it pharmacy related?

Maj. Reyes: In Afghanistan I was the policy lead advisor. The job is basically to mentor the program lead for the Afghan National Army to develop the pharmacy technician curriculum and program. We helped them develop a new curriculum. Basically, after the combat mission in Afghanistan, it was switched to a mentoring mission to establish a sustainability of the Afghan National Army for them to be able to fight on their own, to do things on their own. The mandate for the mission was to help them establish themselves for sustainability so I was mentoring the lead for the allied health profession in the Afghan Forces Academy of Medical Science (AFAMS). Alongside doctors, nurses, dentist, physiotherapist, preventative medicine group, physician assistant and the leadership, we basically mentored our counterparts in the Afghan National Army. We did it alongside with the US group as well. The US group usually mentors the hospitals but I do go in as well in the hospital to check on how we're gonna integrate the changes in the program with what they needed in actual practice. There's a lot of curriculum development involved, a lot of gathering information, a lot of interviewing and making sure that what we are proposing or what we plan to implement would really be applicable to the setting because our practices are different from theirs, they're just starting on the very basic. They don't have much knowledge and that's the biggest challenge as well. I mean there's always that cultural barrier with us and them specially the language. I would always use a translator but not all information were translated properly so that's one of the bigger challenge and even the course materials, the lectures, the curriculum we had a hard time having it translated because they're too technical for the translator to do. So that's basically what I did in Afghanistan.

Kathryn: Being an immigrant to Canada, did it post any problem when you were in the army or in general, not just in the army. What were the challenges?

Maj. Reyes: You know, there's always this hardship. You can't really get away without having one. It's not even trying to fit in to the Canadian population or Canadian way of life. Not even that, there's that moments of isolation and all. It's just so different. Nothing too big really, even in the military. Military in Canada is really good in terms of welcoming other races. We promote those things. We promote diversity. We encourage people or the visible minorities to join just to basically have that good mix and good representation as well.

Kathryn: When you were training, are there also people with different backgrounds or other immigrants as well?

Maj. Reyes: A couple of us probably 4 or 5 of us. The thing is when you come to Canada or when you do those things, you have to expect that you would have to adapt to the norm to what's there you see. You shouldn't expect that they would adjust for you.

Kathryn: Was it difficult for you to adjust or you were able to handle it well?

Maj. Reyes: Yeah, I didn't have any issue. Everybody goes through the same thing anyway, so I guess it's really the understanding that it's normal. The thought should be to go into doing something, not expecting any extraordinary from other people. Extraordinary treatment or anything like that. If really you want equality, then you should treat everybody with that thought. If you want to be treated equally then you should think that everybody should be treated equally as well and no special favors, special attention given to you because you're not from here.

Kathryn: Did you experience any discrimination?

Maj. Reyes: Nope. You are only discriminated if you allow them to. Don't give them reason to discriminate you.

Kathryn: Aside from trying to fit in, are there any more challenges personally or within yourself that you have to kind of talk to yourself?

Maj. Reyes: Well, it isn't really about being different or not being originally from here. The whole job itself, it's hard even if you're from here you'd experience the same thing. There are times that you just have to bear with it and you know that everything is okay. There's always a light by the end of the tunnel.

Kathryn: What helped you overcome challenges?

Maj. Reyes: Us Filipinos we're very resilient to changes, we're very resilient in dealing with adversities. We've been pretty much, I shouldn't say trained, but we are, to react to those kinds of things. So that helps. Having that kind of training beforehand in the Philippines of being resilient helped you in dealing with difficulties and new challenges that comes with your job, I think that is actually a trait that most Filipinos share and I think that is what makes Filipinos flourish.

Kathryn: Can you share a little bit what attitude or what helped you become successful? What helped you achieve those goals that you have?

Maj. Reyes: First of all, you always have to have a goal. Always have a plan in your head on how you can achieve that. You will not succeed on your goal if you don't have a plan on how to achieve it. Be flexible. Me, being in the military or even going back to me coming to Canada, I kind of want to be here but I should have a plan as well in case things don't work out. I didn't have much back then, but I figured it out even in the military if I didn't succeed in doing the task given to me or the things being thrown at me, then if I didn't plan or didn't think about it, then I wouldn't succeed. There's always as well perseverance, good analysis of the situation. To me, I always do options analysis. I know it's not a common thing to do, but I do that. If you have to have options, you have to do options analysis. You can't be stuck on one single thing and you can't put all your eggs to that basket, because what if it doesn't go, then at least you're prepared and you're not so frustrated, you don't get stuck with it.

Kathryn: Can you say you are a natural optimist or a realist?

Maj. Reyes: Both, because optimism comes with realism.

Kathryn: What is your advice to other immigrants?

Maj. Reyes: Perseverance pays of in the end. Just be flexible and adaptable to change. One of our motto in the military is "adapt and overcome" and that's what I've been doing all along, to adapt and overcome. This job, even if I tell you, you don't even know what I do, you can't even imagine how I do it, because coming from our background back home, that's not something that we do and we know. So yes, adapt and overcome.

Chistina (Tina) Privado, RPh
Pharmacy Owner , Sandycove Drug Store – Barrie, ON
Business Partner, Rainbow Pharmasave – Angus, ON,
Memorial Pharmasave – Orillia, ON, Schomberg Village
Pharmacy – Schomberg, ON

Kathryn: Can you tell me about yourself, how you come into this country and the beginning of your journey?

Tina: Zellers company was looking for pharmacists in Philippines because at that time they were kind of struggling to fill pharmacist positions in their stores. Zellers contacted someone who had a connection in the Philippines. A friend encouraged me to try but at that point in time in the Philippines there have been a lot of reports and stories as well about recruiters who are just making money out of people. It's very challenging at first to really see if it's true and really commit to it because I did't want to be part of a scam where I spend all that money and nothing happens. But the procedure, the process on how to get to there it made the opportunity look more legitimate because I had to go to a screening process and pass a screening exam in Philippines before being accepted to be eligible to apply for the Pharmacy Examining Board of Canada (PEBC) Evaluating Examination in Vancouver. Passing the evaluating exam is a requirement to become a candidate for PEBC Qualifying exam in both written (MCQ) and oral form (OSCE). I came back to Philippines to wait for the results and then waited again until the papers are approved. It took about another year or so before I was able to get a visa and come here Canada as a student sponsored by Zellers company.

Kathryn: What did you have to give up in the Philippines for you to come here?

Tina: There were a lot of considerations of course. I had a good job in the Philippines, I taught in a university and at that time and just finished my master's degree. I actually started enrolling for a doctorate degree in pharmacy, I took maybe few courses already. I've been in the university for 5 or 6 years at that time and I really enjoyed what I was doing as a faculty member of the school of pharmacy in Centro Escolar University. It was a very respectable job, so that is one thing. The second thing was my family. Right after I took the PEBC exam my father passed away, so he was not there to see it through. I'm thankful but I had to give up that sense of belongingness with my family. Coming to Canada, I did't know anybody and felt so isolated and so alone in a foreign country and I did't know what my future holds. But you have to have that kind of hope that something good is coming out of the decision that you make.

Kathryn: Did you have a dream of what is it that propelled you to make the decision to come?

Tina: One is, I want to make something better for myself for my family and growing up in a small town in a small island, I always kind of dreamt and kind of envious of people that I knew as a child I was always like 'maybe one day I hope I'll be able to go to America'.

Kathryn: You entered the International Pharmacy Program and then you became a pharmacist. What are the uncertainties that you had?

Tina: Every step of the way in every stage towards becoming a pharmacist there were many uncertainties. Let's say for example as you go into the program, are you going to be able to make it through the program, are you cut out for that? When you pass the Canadian Pharmacist Skills bridging programs I & II and you did your internship, now you have to take the exam, will you be able to pass the exam? You are tested in terms of your ability to demonstrate the competencies that you learned from your written exam. You have to demonstrate if you are really practicing and engaging with the patient. For most people like me including, that's very nerve wracking and very challenging because even if you know those theories and you know what to say but when you're in that situation when someone is giving you a certain scenario and someone is assessing you right in front of you and every time he's trying to mark down something once you open your mouth, it is very intimidating and you get so nervous and maybe you won't be able to apply what you've actually learned. But thankfully, I was able to make it in those exams but then again, challenges never ends.

Kathryn: Part of the challenge of an immigrant pharmacist when you come to Canada and when you take those exams, there's always this thought that, oh my gosh what if I don't pass, I don't have my family, I'll incurred all this debt. What am I going to do?

Tina: That is definitely true. Passing the exam means you can stay in the country but if you don't pass the exam you have to go back to your country so that's going to be very devastating and embarrassing and what about all the money that you owed Zellers for trying to get you here, the loan that they lend you for you to be able to live here, for your rent, for your food, payment for all the exams? I think because you have all those thoughts in your head it can go both ways. It can give you a driving force to make sure you try as hard as you can, to make sure you do well, because there's no alternative. The other thing, as an immigrant you always have to kind of work harder than anyone else to prove that you can be a better candidate than the other candidates.

Kathryn: It doesn't stop there, when you're a student and when you become a pharmacist you continue to have to prove yourself.

Tina: I'm not sure if you want to do it to prove to yourself or you want to prove something to other people. I find that as an immigrant, let's say practitioner, I try to prove myself that yes, I may be an immigrant but I can be a better. I don't know if it's a good comparison but yes, you can be a better or maybe the best practitioner. Even if you're an immigrant that you want to always be the better than the best. You don't want to be like anybody else because as an immigrant knows….you try to prove to someone I guess that "I am better or I am the best". There's always that kind of sort of thinking that I don't know if it's just for myself or other people who immigrated as well maybe have that kind of thought as well. For example, trying to prove to your employer and there are 3 or 4 candidates why would you choose me above other candidates who are not immigrants. I know we have equal opportunity. Definitely, if you are the Human Resource person hiring an employee, you're going to have to take into account their qualifications. What would make them hire me, an immigrant as oppose to those three other people. That's why you want to prove yourself that you're the better or the best.

Kathryn: I think that's our driving force and that's why a lot of us became successful.

Tina: It definitely helps. We also did not come here alone. Even if you still feel kind of alone because your family is not there but I think there are other people who are in the same situation as you that came here. So, it kind of gives us support because you're not the only one who's going through it like there are 20 other pharmacists who are in the same situation as you are and you try to kind of help each other and maybe substitute that sense of like the family that you are longing for because they're not here so basically those people who came with you becomes part of your family.

Kathryn: In terms of cultural differences, have you experienced challenges?

Tina: There is always that cultural differences but the way I see it is, I came to this country, I am an immigrant, I have my own beliefs, I have my own views, I have my own culture. But at the same time people who are here have their own beliefs, culture, traditions and practices as well, so I have two options it's either enforce what I have, or try to adapt to what is in here and I think there's nothing wrong with either or except that for myself I chose to adapt to the culture that they have here. I'm not saying I'm forgetting what I had before but I wanna be able to fit in. I wanna be able to adapt to the culture and the practices that they have in here. So for me, I don't really find it as a challenge. It will be challenging if you are more resistant to change. I didn't really see it as an obstacle. It depends on your mindset. If you want to resist that cultural shift or you want to be able to adapt and maybe there could be a good thing about it and it's up to you how you're going to use it.

Kathryn: What are other barriers to success that you have experienced?

Tina: I couldn't say they are barriers because if they are barriers, I wouldn't be where I am right now. Being a female gender sometimes can be viewed as a barrier to success. I'm not saying I never had that kind of feeling that you're not good enough or maybe, that feeling that you're a little bit kind of a failure, you're a little guy, you're a little person. When I started with Zellers as an employee I just followed my boss, followed whatever the protocols they had, and I always say it doesn't matter if you don't own it, you just try the best that you can and practiced in my best capability. But it all kind of changed a little bit of course when I moved from the corporate to an independent pharmacy. At that time, I was given a very small percentage of the shares in the company, to be part of it. My partners were men and I'm the only female partner. They were very helpful. One of my partner's, became my mentor and he showed me a lot of ways in order to succeed. When I was starting 10 or 12 years ago, sometimes I had a feeling that because I'm a female I don't know if I can make it, you know, when talking to men in business meetings. Pharmacy business was a male dominated business before. I just felt like that at first. It's something that I had at that time. It's something that I had to overcome. It doesn't matter whatever gender you are we can all succeed. But the lesson is for you, that if such feelings linger, you don't let that be a hindrance or a barrier to achieve something. And in my case, I did not. I had that feeling at first but it's a matter of overcoming that feeling.

Kathryn: From your journey as a pharmacist employee to becoming a business owner now - you own four pharmacy businesses, what mindset shift had to happen within yourself that you find difficult at first?

Tina: One is that I guess as a person, it's really in you whether you're a hardworking person or not. An owner or being an employee, I don't think would change that. I'm always a person who works hard. It didn't matter whether I was an employee I still worked hard the way I worked hard when I was already a part owner of a store. I think one of the reasons why my partners before kept me and offered me more percentage was that even if I only had a small percentage of the store, I still took it as if I owned the whole store. I think there is a difference in the mindset when you say "oh, I only own a little bit of percentage so I will only work a little bit". For me, I took it as if this is my store. It doesn't matter how much you own, this is my store and I wanna make sure it runs very well and I wanna make sure it becomes profitable I still want to work hard with whatever percentage I have.

So that's one thing that still didn't change. When you're an employee, you just follow whatever they want you to do. But when you're a business owner, that changes everything because now you're gonna have to be directly involved in terms of how you want to run the business. It's not just practicing based on your profession as a pharmacist but there's another component to it. It's challenging because you have to learn it. It's not something that you learn from school. I didn't go to business school. To get started with it is very challenging. I wished they have some sort of crash course in the university kind of incorporated before in terms of pharmacy management that could give us a foundation in terms of that aspect of the business when owning a pharmacy. I'm glad I have my partners as well that showed me how and gave me directions on how to properly and profitably run the business. It's a business and at the same time I'm still a health care professional so I make sure there is that kind of balance as well. Ever since I started, I always made sure that the business comes second, the profession still have to come first. At the end of the day we still have to act on the best interest of the patients. I always make sure that the business takes a back seat and I have to focus on the professional aspect.

Kathryn: Did you have fears when you jumped from being an employee to a business owner?

Tina: Yes, because I know there's gonna be more responsibility you know. When my contract with Zellers finished, I had an option of staying with Zellers or venture into this new adventure of partly owning a business and running it. At the same time, it's a different type of responsibility and I do have some concerns at first because I was all settled with Zellers as well. I've been there for three years and kind of getting used to it. I thought I don't even know how this pharmacy works why do I want to move when I'm already settled? I already knew all the patients and was quite happy with where I was at that point in time. So, what's in it in me to take that kind of risk? In my life, I always took risks but maybe more like calculated risks. If I lose, I can go back to work as a pharmacist. I'm not gonna be an employee forever, and that for me is the reward that I was looking forward to. At the same time there is more growth potential for me by owning as oppose to being an employee because as an employee I'm dictated in what I can do. As an owner, I have the flexibility on how I want to get things done and how I want to run my pharmacy.

Kathryn: Have you always been business minded?

Tina: Growing up, we were so poor. Looking back, I cannot imagine myself that I'm gonna be here. Comparing my life then and my life now, I always remember that we were always struggling growing up. We didn't have new clothes, new shoes, we didn't have electronics, we didn't have those when we were growing up. We had to work hard. My parents had to work hard to feed us. We made homemade stuff with my mom like pickled papaya after school or on the weekend. We made that and put it in jars and I will knock on our neighbor's doors and I would sell it. My dad would buy fish in bulk and we would sell it, my sister and me. When I was in elementary school I would buy food in bulk and I would sell it in school so I would make more money. Now looking back at myself at an early age, I can really sell something to be able to make money. It's out of necessity that I have to do it that time but I guess that's the foundation. I didn't know I was learning to sell since I did it at an early age.

Kathryn: I guess part of the reason that made you successful in this business is because you already had that strength and then you just found it out later on that you can actually do it. In between finding that strength, that period when you are fearful, you didn't know that was your strength you didn't know that you were going to be successful.

Tina: You have to be tested first to find out you have that, sometimes you are presented a situation and only at that time that you're presented with a situation that you actually kind of have a self-discovery moment when you say, "Oh, I can actually do it! I can make it happen".

Kathryn: When you think about it, there are opportunities out there. It's just you stepping out for yourself and seeing if you can do it and not be afraid and even though you're afraid, just try it.

Tina: It's human nature to feel some sort of fear. Fear is kind of healthy in a way 'cuz its kind of your guard but utilizing that fear to your advantage. Yes, you have that kind of worry, sometimes doubt or fear the 'what if' in life in whatever decision and choices you make. Given all those, if there is something that you could do, one, you still win and the other portion is if it fails. So that's the A option. What if the option A does not work what's gonna be your option B if the plan A fails, or what's gonna be the plan C if plan B actually fails.

Kathryn: So that fear can serve as your guide to make strategies for success basically.

Tina: It makes you learn from. It's not something that's prescribed for you. Its not something that's been handed out for you. You have to really dig deep into yourself as to how are you going to make it work even if that option A fails because it makes you explore other possibilities. You can explore other possibilities - other opportunities that could lead to you reaching those goals even if that first option fails or didn't work out.

Kathryn: Do you enjoy what you're doing?

Tina: It is very challenging. It is very stressful. Anything that involves decision you always have to think hard about it. For me, I still love what I do. There might be a mess in here, maybe so much things to prepare and I'm tired but I still enjoy it. I still get satisfaction from it. I still enjoy what I'm doing despite of all the work involved. At the end of the day, when I get something accomplished like a certain project, I still get the feeling of accomplishment that I made it through after all the delays, the challenges, at the end it's so rewarding.

Kathryn: What is more rewarding to you, the business side or the pharmacy practitioner side?

Tina: I would say both. It's a balance between the two. Like what I said earlier, I still want to put my professional practice first and for me that's very important because the business side kind of follows as well. I think the majority of my patients come to the pharmacy because of the service that people find my pharmacy. It's that kind of connection that I have with my patients and I think for me that's very rewarding to see. The business side comes after because if you can keep those people, that kind of loyalty, your patients no matter what, they will come to you. At the same time if they are happy and they are satisfied with the service you provide in them, they're the ones who will be your great ambassadors and outside in the community to get more referrals and other people to come to your pharmacy as well. The business side always follows if you practice the best that you can practice.

Kathryn: Are you satisfied with where you are right now?

Tina: There are so much that have happened already in the 16 years of my life that I'm here that I would never imagined to have happened maybe fifteen or twenty years ago. I'm kind of settled now but it doesn't mean it ends there. As what I've said earlier there's always that constant opportunity.

Kathryn: Are you constantly evaluating where you are now to where you could be or you just take it one step at a time when opportunity comes?

Tina: We always dream, and we always want to be the better of where you are, what you are right now. For me, I don't wanna just stop in here. You challenge yourself maybe ten years down the road I wanna be this, I wanna have that. You still have to have a goal to yourself that maybe five years, ten years down the road, for me, if I get there, I'm good. If I don't get it, I'm good as well. But I envision myself in five years, in ten years, this is where I wanna be, this is what I wanna have, this is who I want to be. If it happens, I'm going to be very grateful. If it doesn't happen, it's very great the way I have it right now. I am not going to make that kind of define how I live my life now. I don't want to be too disappointed that it never happened. But then again, that vision in five or ten years later will that define, dictate who I am right now? No, I don't want that to happen because I don't want to be consumed by my goals 5 to 10 years down the road and not be able to live with what I have right now. For me I always have goals, five to ten years later but I don't want that to prevent me from living on what is the present. *Kathryn:* The goals that you set for yourself, had those goals happened for you?

Tina: Most of them did.

Kathryn: What's your advice to other immigrants?

Tina: There are a few tips I could impart to them based from what I've learned. One is, you have to be resilient. It doesn't mean if something didn't work out the first time, you give up, because there's always a second time, there's always the third time. You have to be resilient. The other thing is, always try to do the best that you can in every situation. Give your 110% always no matter what the situation is. You may not find yourself rewarded at that time that you are doing that but at the end you'll always be rewarded for your hardwork. Hardwork, resilience, and never give up. Life doesn't transition in an instant. It is a process. It is a process and even after now my life is still in process. There's a continuous struggle about something, continuous challenges, continuous opportunities and it's up to me to either take on all those challenges or maybe just stop from there but I don't think that's my personality to just stop at a certain point.

Rajesh Mehta, RPh
Pharmacy Manager/Pharmacy Owner
Senior Marketing Director World Financial Group

Kathryn: Hi Rajesh, thanks for agreeing to this interview. Can you tell me a little bit about yourself and your journey?

Rajesh: I did my Bachelor's in Pharmacy in 1979 and was University lecturer in India. I came to Montreal and learned that it takes three years to learn French and write the exam in French. I quit the company and decided to move to Toronto. This is the first time in my life I quit. I got a call in Montreal for an interview and I got the job as a Quality Control Director with 200 people under me. They provided me with translator, but I did not think I could learn French that fast, so I told them to look for another person and I came to Toronto.

I came to Toronto, Ontario College of Pharmacists asked me to go back to school. At that time, there were three subjects you had to do, Pharmacology, Medicinal Chemistry and Pharmacokinetics. I had a Master's in Pharmaceutical Chemistry, Medicinal Chemistry but they said it does not matter whether you had a PhD or not you still had to go and study.

I did TOEFL in 1979 but they said I had to do the TOEFL again. I told them that I did TOEFL then I taught in University in English then I came here so does my English improved or did it deteriorate? They told me it does not matter you still had to do that. I went to the university with a hundred twenty students, none of them had knowledge with practicals.

Our first exam in Medicinal Chemistry, there were two questions and I wrote my answers. Later on, the teacher called me to the office and asked me, "Who are you?". Well, I said I am Rajesh Mehta and I have a Master's degree in Medicinal Chemistry. He told me you should not be here. You should get the license. I said, one bureaucrat told me to go and do this and another one told me I should have a license. What is going on? I finished one year Medicinal Chemistry and Pharmacokinetics then wrote the school exam with good marks. Second year, I studied Pharmacology and wrote the PEBC exam and passed.

After the license, I did training in an apothecary in Scarborough from 5pm to 1 am. When I worked some people would tell me why I could not read the name because the doctor's writing is illegible. Then I became bold and thought nobody should harass me anymore. One time I called the doctor to clarify a prescription and he asked me why I don't know that, where I came from, where did I study. I said, doctor I called you so that the patient's health can be taken care of. I don't want to give the wrong medication and what is wrong in calling you? You cannot tell what it is that you are writing instead of asking me where I graduated and all that? He should have been thanking me for taking care of his patients.

I decided to open my own pharmacy and have my own business. It was very difficult for six months with one prescription a day then two prescriptions a day then it started growing then I had three Zellers franchise pharmacies, one in Scarborough and two in Mississauga. It was good business. I thought I would retire with those businesses but then one day Zellers announced that they were closing the store. It was a big bombshell, sort of like a heart attack. What will happen to my store? I was told to pay to keep the files otherwise thy would sell the store.

They wanted the money and the signed agreement within 24 hours. I had money coming from the previous month and I told them keep that as a deposit and I am going to get the rest tomorrow, keep that money for 3 months, together with the consecutive months until the day we close in 3 months and then you will get the rest on the closing date, not before that. So they agreed and I closed that store and move here to this location on the 15 of October 2007, 3 ½ km apart from the original store but I lost a lot of customers 50% of my customers because seniors can't come since it takes about 3 buses to come here.

I lost a lot of business but still I didn't get scared. I kept on running and running and all these years, together with the financial depressions and the markets crashing the banks and everybody kept on taking advantage of me asking me to keep on shifting money from here to there and everywhere the money doesn't grow for me, but they make money.

I was interested on to sell and grow my money in the stock market. I lost millions over the years until one day I joined in to this world financial group to see what can I do in that. I learned a lot about insurances RSPS & ESPS and all that. All of these happened in 2013. I was just studying not doing anything and in 2015 I got the licensed. I started approaching people investing their money and getting them insurances and all that, helping them to save money and make their money grow. That helped me. I am doing that combined with the pharmacy, doing income taxes for people, tons of things all sort of financial-related techniques and God knows what else I can do.

Pretty much making money, I made 57K last year of WFG and I went from a simple agent to senior marketing director now even opening my office, I just signed the lease last week opening in May 2018.

Kathryn: From lecturer to pharmacist then to insurance agent to Senior Marketing Director for WFG, they are all very different.

Rajesh: In 1979, I was making products and was a chemist then went into research then did the masters then worked in the university as a lecturer then came here then I studied and then the business and then another business… plenty of things.

When I first came here, I stayed with few people first and earn some money. One bedroom apartment costs four hundred and fifty dollars back then but I had only twenty dollars. I did not have enough money, not even for a month, not even enough for a day. So I had to work whatever. I had people at that time who took responsibility to be a guarantor for me because without a job nobody would rent you an apartment.

Kathryn: What kind of work did you do when you first came here?

Rajesh: All kinds of jobs. I did clothing, clothes-stitching, shoe-stitching. Even in today's time, I don't have a cleaner in my pharmacy. I do the cleaning myself. I do all kinds of job.

Kathryn: What is it that keeps you going?

Rajesh: I don't know, I just want to learn every single thing. My father was a teacher - teaching students in small houses. There were the students sitting in one room and I am sitting in the other room then my father told me that I need to learn everything be a jack of everything, so I always say I am a jack of all trades master of pharmacy. Now I am jack of all, master of pharmacy and insurance.

Kathryn: That's really good!

Rajesh: I have taxes to be done for myself and for other people, I just like to keep busy I can't sit and wait. Monday to Friday I think of Sunday and when Sunday comes I think, ummm…. I have this work to do. I do everything I can do, carpeting, electricity, plumbing, drywalling all of it.

Kathryn: So, you are all-around.

Rajesh: Yeah, last Sunday I was in the attic doing insulation

Kathryn: You went through a lot of difficulties and you said you are not scared. What is that which keeps you from being scared of trying?

Rajesh: I am not scared of anything I will try anything.

Kathryn: Is it something that you grew up with? Is it something that you learned from your parents?

Rajesh: Yeah, I learned from my parents yes. Nobody is perfect on the first day, and you better try every different things to be perfect. Like when I was born I was not a pharmacist. I learned something, I went into science and learned science then I went into the pharmacy course and I became a pharmacist. If I go into accounting I can become an accountant, or electrician or doctor or anything.

Kathryn: Ah! I see!

Rajesh: I just try it! Give me a shot and I will study it with my whole heart.

Kathryn: Right, because some people have a fixed mindset.

Rajesh: No, no, no, no...

Kathryn: A fixed mindset that says, I am going to be like this for the rest of my life!

Rajesh: I will never be like that you know, see....ahhh... when you came and worked with me in 2004.

Kathryn: Yes, 2004

Rajesh: I was diagnosed with a brain tumor. I was operated, I was worried and still I was working until 9PM in Zellers and after that I was doing deliveries until 11PM then I called one of my best friends. He came to the apartment and then I told him that tomorrow 5AM I will be undergoing surgery. When I reached home I was writing my will in case I do not come back tomorrow. But I had my faith, I had my God that I will be back and I came back then the doctor told me before the surgery that I needed to take six months of time off. Six months time-off in pharmacy is very difficult then I would be in the ICU for a week. After the operation went by, I woke up at 2AM and the nurse kept on asking me many different questions, and I answered everything. She told me that I will be in ICU for a week but I was out of ICU the next morning. After the ICU, I was in the changing room with three other people and my gosh... I was the only one who could walk or talk. So,I did not look forward to staying in that environment. I can't handle that. I walked, exercised and was discharged in the 5th day after the operation, I reached home.

Kathryn: You had the will....

Rajesh: I just wanted to get out, they told me "DON'T EVEN TRY IT!" and this was on 23rd of September 2004 when I was operated. I was home at the end of September and by October 2nd my father in law died so I had to go to the funeral. My wife doesn't drive in the 401 and I said ok get the car out of the garage and I drove the car to the funeral in downtown

Kathryn: Was your vision okay?

Rajesh: My vision was okay, but I was not able to move my head, I just looked in the mirror. In today's time they can operate me here (pointing to an area on his head) without anesthesia. It is solid tumor but I lost my hearing on my right side. I lost it since 2004, so that's why the pharmacy counter is this way so the customer stands on my left side so I can hear him.

Kathryn: Oh... I did not know that...

Rajesh: I just keep it like that so I can hear them. If you are on my right, not a word goes in my ear I can't hear it.

Kathryn: Where you able to eat after the operation?

Rajesh: Yes, liquids. My wife kept on massaging me and I massaged as well. I drank lots of coconut water to heal faster. Six weeks after the operation I was in the pharmacy working twelve hours a day. In November, I started working twelve hours.

Kathryn: Was that hard for your body?

Rajesh: I was okay.

Kathryn: You love pharmacy that's why.

Rajesh: I just love my customers, I love my pharmacy. That's the reason.

Kathryn: Maybe that helped you heal faster.

Rajesh: Yeah, oh yeah. After Zellers closed that's what kept me going. First it was like a heart attack right? I can just close the store and not open another store and go work somewhere and still make eighty thousand dollars. At that time, it was not that hard but because the love of my customers and my faith in my God.

What would they think? They'll think "Rajesh left us. He is nowhere to be found", so I said okay whatever happens, happens for the good. With my God, I opened the pharmacy. The pharmacy was closed October 2007. That year in March 2007, I had bought a new house and the closing of that was 2008 of February. I had borrowed one million dollars from the bank to pay for the house, to pay for the Zellers and to pay for the construction of this pharmacy. In my mind it's trouble, right? But I was like it's okay. I paid back one million dollars in one year. I cleared my debt. It is the love of my customers that kept me going, even today.

Kathryn: I remembered you had a hard time when you started here.

Rajesh: My family was the most important thing. They have always supported me. They would wait for me until eleven o'clock and twelve o'clock at night, they never argued. They knew that I do it for them. Even today I always keep myself busy. They were always there for me, all of them.

Kathryn: You like helping people. Ever since I met you, you always have students.

Rajesh: Oh yeah, I don't know how many, maybe around 50 students have become pharmacists.

Kathryn: So you like passing on your knowledge.

Rajesh: Yeah. I always teach whatever I know that can help them you know? I like to share my knowledge. I don't charge anybody for my knowledge. I help them.

Kathryn: Those students that you've helped, have they come back to you?

Rajesh: Yeah, I have one right in front of me (laughs)… after fourteen years, she is right here (referring to Kathryn). Every student, anywhere they are they call.

Kathryn: You keep a large network of people, right?

Rajesh: Yeah.

Kathryn: A very large network and I think that is one of the secrets to your success in the insurance business and the pharmacy field. You genuinely care for them.

Rajesh: Yeah, whether they buy from me or not. I will grow old and once I am 80 years old if I have not passed my knowledge that means that when it is my time, the person serving me does not know properly right? So it is actually to my benefit that I pass my knowledge because tomorrow, I'm gonna need them.

Kathryn: I have never heard of that before but that is really cool.

Rajesh: That's what I was always thinking, that the world is very small. If I do bad things to people, then tomorrow that bad thing is gonna come to me.

Kathryn: Right, yeah.

Rajesh: If I point one finger at you, three fingers are pointing at me. I have not taught you, who looks bad right? I don't want to be remembered like that. I want to be remembered that I did the right thing. I try to do my best, helping others.

Kathryn: Have you ever had a problem with how people perceive you other than the discrimination you experienced when you first started?

Rajesh: No, after the first three years of working in the pharmacy I developed enough confidence. When I had my Zellers pharmacy, my customers will only fill prescriptions with me even though there are other pharmacies around.

Kathryn: What is it that you do that makes people trust you?

Rajesh: I don't know. I try to be nice. I try to help them. I have a customer 50 kilometers away and I drove and delivered his prescription. I have a customer who just texted me to fill her prescription. She lives over an hour's drive from here. I'm going to deliver her prescription after I close the pharmacy before I go home.

Kathryn: Wow, that is over and beyond good customer service. Why do you serve like that?

Rajesh: I don't know why but I've been doing like that since my birth, in India. We always had visitors and other people. It's what I learned from the beginning in India. It's not something that I learned in Canada but from the beginning. My father was a teacher, my mother came from a millionaire family. My grandfather, my mother's father, he worked for the king. He worked sort of like CEO in a king's kingdom, so I have seen the golden plates, the golden sort of containers to store the food and the diamond cutters and all that. Two hundred diamond cutters working in our house. The house, it was like a palace then everything was lost when my grandfather passed away. He had so much money that we didn't have to work but then everything was lost. Time changes everything, right? My mother had so many relatives, cousins and all so it was lost. My father was teaching and there were a lot of students who could not even afford, there were a lot of people in the society that you pay for their tuition to make them study. We helped them, whatever we could. So many people we helped out so I have seen all these. It comes in my blood.

Kathryn: You have given so much to so many people. That is why I want to feature you.

Rajesh: I went to Whistler for a WFG convention and I won an award. I travel a lot now. I also went to Las Vegas then came back directly to pharmacy, I did not even come home.

Kathryn: (laughs) That is dedication to your customers.

Rajesh: Wherever I am today, it is because of my customers. They have been faithful to me. From their home to here, there could be two hundred pharmacies and they can go to any pharmacy but they come to me. I have one customer who is in Ottawa (about four hours and thirty-minute drive from Toronto). She sends her daughter to pick up medication only from me. Once in awhile, I end up going there. If they are taking the trouble to come to me, once in awhile no problem, call me anytime.

Kathryn: What advice would you give to other immigrants?

Rajesh: You know, don't be scared. Nowadays there's a lot of technology if you don't know. There's a lot of information at the tip of your fingers. Work hard, that the most important thing. Take any kind of job and then look for work in your field. Then you have to learn, go to school and update your knowledge, pass the exams here. Sometimes it can take years.

Kathryn: Rajesh, thank you so much for sharing your journey with me today.

End of interviews.

An Encouragement...

Dear reader,

Thank you for taking the time to read this book. In your quest for success, remember to be grateful, always...for what you have now and what had already been accomplished in your life. Thank yourself, thank the people who have helped you get there. Most of all, thank God for the gift of life and allowing you to make a difference in other peoples' lives. I hope that you live a life not only of success but of significance.

Remember that you matter....
Dream high and dream BIG!!!!

May God bless you in your endeavors.

Your friend,
Kathryn

References

1. The Artisan Soul, Erwin McManus, TEDx Hongkong

2. http://www.psychmechanics.com/2014/08/beliefs-programs-of-subconscious-mind.html 1

3. https://www.ncbi.nlm.nih.gov/pmc/articles/PMC2802367/ 2

4. Quantum: A Guide to The Perplexed by Al Khalili

5. Dr. Leaf, Caroline. Switch On Your Brain. The Key to Peak Happiness, Thinking, and Health. Michigan: Baker Books, 2013.

6. en.wikipedia.org/wiki/Force_multiplication

7. https://www.bls.gov/careeroutlook/2015/article/wage-differences.htm

8. Robbins, Tony. The Power of State. Unlimited Power. The New Science of Personal Achievement. NewYork: Free Press, 2003. P. 38

9. O'Connor, Joseph & John Seymour. Introducing (NLP) Nero-Linguistic Programming. Psychological Skills for Understanding and Influencing People. London: Element, 2002. P 19-21

10. Cabane, Olivia Fox. The Charisma Myth. How Anyone Can Master the Art and Science of Personal Magnetism. New York: Penguin Group, 2013. P. 98-114

11. Spencer, E. (2009). It's All About the People: Cultural Intelligence (CQ) as a Force Multiplier in the Contemporary Operating Environment. *The Journal of Conflict Studies, 29*(0). Retrieved 4 8, 2018, from https://journals.lib.unb.ca/index.php/jcs/article/view/15235/19648

www.ingramcontent.com/pod-product-compliance
Lightning Source LLC
Chambersburg PA
CBHW022044190326
41520CB00008B/697